A YEAR OF

TAOISM

DAILY WISDOM AND MEDITATIONS FOR A LIFE OF BALANCE

ELIZABETH RENINGER

ROCKRIDGE
PRESS

To my teachers and friends along the Way.

First Rockridge Press trade paperback edition 2022

Rockridge Press and the Rockridge Press logo are trademarks or registered trademarks of Callisto Media Inc. and/or its affiliates in the United States and other countries and may not be used without written permission.

For general information on our other products and services, please contact our Customer Care Department within the United States at (866) 744-2665, or outside the United States at (510) 253-0500.

Paperback ISBN: 978-1-68539-729-6
eBook ISBN: 979-8-88608-816-8

Manufactured in the United States of America

Interior and Cover Designer: John Calmeyer
Art Producer: Melissa Melinowksy
Editor: Charlie Duerr
Production Editor: Jaime Chan
Production Manager: Martin Worthington

All illustrations used under license from Shutterstock

10 9 8 7 6 5 4 3 2 1 0

A YEAR OF TAOISM

CONTENTS

INTRODUCTION

Welcome to *A Year of Taoism*!

Here you'll find explorations and exercises drawn from the Taoist tradition that you can experiment with on your own. You'll also find reflections and inquiries to inspire and deepen your understanding, and support the discovery of a peace, joy, and freedom that surpasses all understanding. Among the practices and reflections are quotes from the *Tao Te Ching* and other notable Taoist adepts: words of wisdom to contemplate and cherish.

If you're new to Taoism, this book will offer a glimpse into the vast terrain of this ancient spiritual tradition. If you're already familiar with Taoist practice, you'll likely find (and hopefully enjoy) some new opportunities to refine your understanding and render your human body-mind more fully transparent to the Light of Tao.

My first engagement with Taoist practices came while I was studying Chinese medicine. My course of study included *ch'i-kung*—a form of Taoist yoga with roots in ancient China—and its practice has been part of my life ever since. The Taoist celebration of the natural world, its appreciation of spontaneity and paradox, and its invitation to live life in deep harmony with the flowing patterns of the universe are principles that I continue to value and do my best to embody.

I look forward to serving as your guide, introducing exercises and inquiries with immediate relevance to your daily life, and the harmony of our shared planet.

KEY TAOIST TERMS

Some Chinese terms, relevant to Taoist practice, that you'll find in this book include:

ch'i (also spelled *qi*): subtle life-force energy

ch'i-kung (also spelled *qigong*): life-force cultivation; body, mind, and breath exercises

feng-shui: the art and science of arranging natural or man-made objects to foster health and prosperity

I-Ching (also spelled *Yijing*): a divination tool consulted by tossing coins or throwing yarrow sticks

tan-t'ien (also spelled *dan-tian*): a subtle energy center; in Taoist practice there are three *tan-t'iens*—located in the lower abdomen, the center-chest, and the head

Tao Te Ching (also spelled *Daode Jing*): the primary scripture of Taoism, attributed to Lao Tzu (also spelled Laozi)

ten thousand things: the entities/events of the natural world (i.e., everything you see, hear, taste, smell, feel, or think)

wu-wei: non-volitional action

yin-ch'i: feminine energy

yang-ch'i: masculine energy

Note: All *Tao Te Ching* excerpts are drawn from J. H. McDonald's English translation.

JANUARY

1

JANUARY

NEWBORN

In the beginning, there is the innocence of the newborn: fresh, open, awake.

A natural abundance of playfulness, curiosity, wonder, and awe. Effortless presence and joyful spontaneity.

Can you resurrect your own childlike wisdom—before words, vast and spirit-rich? Can you welcome and joyfully embrace your original nature—the heart of Tao?

Yes.

2

JANUARY

The tallest tree begins as a tiny sprout.
The tallest building starts with one shovel of dirt.
A journey of a thousand miles starts with a single footstep.

TAO TE CHING, **CHAPTER 64**

3

RIDING THE WAVE OF BREATH

1. Sit comfortably, either on a chair or a cushion on the floor.

2. Smile gently, to help relax the muscles in your face, neck, and jaw.

3. Allow your eyes to close, and bring your attention to the movement of your breath—its inhalations and exhalations.

4. Follow the cycles of breathing—inhale, exhale, inhale—like a surfer riding a wave.

5. Make no effort to control or change the breath in any way; just ride the wave, observing its increase and release.

6. Notice how the breath *feels* in your body, in the nose, throat, chest, belly.

7. Continue for five or ten minutes, or longer if you'd like.

4
JANUARY
GATEWAY

Moment by moment, the breathing process links the space inside the body with the space outside the body, drawing in oxygen and releasing carbon dioxide.

For as long as the body is alive, this gateway between "inside" and "outside" remains open.

5
JANUARY
DISCOVERING YOUR TRUE BODY

1. Find a place to sit quietly for a few minutes.

2. Bring your attention to the movement of your breath—its inhalations and exhalations. Ride the wave of the breath, effortlessly, simply observing its natural rhythm.

3. Appreciate the fact that your body's survival depends on this movement of the breath, in and out.

4. Reflect on the fact that your body depends also on water that you drink and upon plants and animals that you ingest as food.

5. There is no real separation. Your true body is the entire cosmos. Appreciate this deeply as you move through your day.

6
JANUARY
—
MIRROR IMAGE

One of Taoism's essential insights is that the *microcosm* of the human body-mind is a mirror image of the *macrocosm* of the entire cosmos.

Can you see how this is true?

7
JANUARY
—
MOST INTIMATE

Your most intimate experience of the body is via physical sensations—how your body feels "from the inside." Notice that this body felt directly is quite different from the body you see reflected in a mirror or the body that you "see" in your mind's eye.

Which is your real body?

8
JANUARY

The Tao is like an empty container:
it can never be emptied and can never be filled.
Infinitely deep, it is the Source of all things.

TAO TE CHING, **CHAPTER 4**

9
JANUARY

INNER SMILE #1

1. Find a quiet place to sit or lie down.

2. Take a few deep, slow breaths, and relax your jaw completely, as if you were saying "ahh."

3. Rest your attention lightly at the center of your forehead; then let it drift back to the very center of your skull, resting your focus gently there.

4. Smile gently, with your entire being as well as your mouth. Feel smile-energy gathering and illuminating your entire head and face.

5. Allow your eyes to become smiling eyes.

6. With smiling eyes, turn your gaze inward, to smile at your heart. Imagine smile-energy gently enveloping your precious human heart.

7. If you have an injury or illness, send smile-energy to that part of your body, infusing it with loving kindness.

10
JANUARY
—
INTERNAL PHARMACY

The simple act of smiling catalyzes a cornucopia of beneficial biochemical changes. Smiling releases endorphins that act as pain relievers, serotonin that acts as an antidepressant, and neuropeptides that provide stress relief.

How wonderful!

11

JANUARY

FLOWER GAZING

1. Sit facing a single flower that is inspiring to you. It can be a cut stem in a vase, a flower blossoming in the wild, or a photograph.

2. Gaze lovingly—with genuine interest and appreciation—at the flower, as though you were greeting a beloved friend.

3. Allow your gaze to become soft and receptive, as though welcoming your good friend into your home for tea.

4. Instead of reaching out to grab the flower with your eyes, invite and fully receive the flower image into your seeing.

5. Feel the intimacy of this soft and receptive way of seeing.

12

JANUARY

COLOR, SHAPE, AND SCENT

Next time you walk through a flower garden or an orchard with its spring blossoms, let yourself be uplifted and amazed by the infinite creativity of the natural world.

What a sublime kaleidoscope of shapes and colors!
What glorious scents!

13
JANUARY
—
PATH OF LEAST RESISTANCE

A stream flowing downward from its source high in the mountains will effort-lessly find the path of least resistance. It won't be a perfectly straight path, but it will be the most efficient one.

Can you do the same?

14
JANUARY
—

The supreme good is like water,
which benefits all of creation
without trying to compete with it.

TAO TE CHING, **CHAPTER 8**

15

JANUARY

AIMLESS WANDERING

Devote some time each day to aimless wandering—moving around without a specific agenda or well-defined goal. Instead, allow your actions to emerge from in-the-moment interest and enthusiasm, from childlike curiosity and playfulness.

Parks, beaches, and forest meadows are excellent for aimless wandering, but any place that's safe and enjoyable is perfect.

Begin by sitting or standing still. Be aware of physical sensations as well as the sights, sounds, and scents of the environment.

When you feel an impulse to move in one direction or another, honor that. When you feel an impulse to pause—for a moment or longer—honor that.

Let yourself move for the simple pleasure of moving rather than as a means to a destination.

That's all.

16
JANUARY
WU-WEI

Wu-wei (non-volitional action) is activity that's a natural expression of the entire universe. In the same way that an ocean wave is a local expression of the whole ocean, the actions of the Taoist sage effortlessly accord with the rhythms of the cosmos.

17
JANUARY
WAYS OF KNOWING

Taoism embraces two ways of knowing:

1. The conceptual knowledge of the thinking mind, and

2. A wisdom that comes from another "dimension." You might call it intuition, apperception, or the "still quiet voice" from the core of your Being.

Become curious about this second way of knowing.

18
JANUARY

CAT AND MOUSE

1. Sit comfortably on either a chair or a cushion on the floor.

2. Gently close your eyes and tune into the movement of the breath—inhale, exhale, inhale, exhale.

3. In the same way that you've been observing the breath, notice the movement of thoughts. See how thoughts arise and dissolve, moment by moment, within the "space" of your mind.

4. Just for fun, imagine that you are a cat waiting patiently next to a mouse-hole. In the same way that the cat watches, with relaxed intensity, for the appearance of a mouse, watch for the appearance of the next thought.

5. Stay with the playful question: *I wonder what my next thought is going to be?*

19
JANUARY

POWERFUL TOOL

The conceptual mind is a wonderfully powerful tool. But just like a hammer is not the right tool for every job, the thinking mind is not always the best tool. Sometimes a softer, more intuitive way of knowing works best.

20
JANUARY

Fishes are born in water. Man is born in Tao. If fishes get ponds to live in, they thrive. If man gets Tao to live in, he may live his life in peace.

—CHUANG TZU (TRANSLATED BY HERBERT GILES)

21
JANUARY
—
FEELING THE *CH'I*

1. Rub the palms of your hands together for fifteen to twenty seconds.

2. Separate your hands just slightly so there's an inch or two of space between the left palm and the right palm.

3. Close your eyes gently, and tune into the sensations in your hands—both the palms and the fingers.

4. Move your hands just slightly—up and down, in circles, or pulsing them a little closer together and farther apart.

5. Feel into the space *between* your palms. Notice sensations both in and around your hands.

6. Sensations of warmth, tingling, heaviness, pulsing, or a magnetic pull are known as *ch'i* sensations—the feeling of life-force energy.

22
JANUARY
—
BREATH AND *CH'I*

When you attend mindfully to your breath, your capacity to feel your body "from inside" will likely be enhanced. This is how the physical breath can be a gateway to an experience of the subtle body—what Taoists refer to as *ch'i* (also spelled *qi*).

23
JANUARY
—
PRACTICE JOURNAL

As a Taoist practitioner, you may find it useful to keep a journal to:

- Track your body-mind cultivation practice.
- Record insights gleaned from meditation and inquiry.
- Note the effects of recent dietary changes.
- Jot down questions that you have.
- Write poems or doodle—expressing creativity.

- Record dreams that feel particularly poignant.
- Collect inspiring quotes from the *Tao Te Ching*.

Tips for keeping a journal:

1. Make it a daily ritual to sit quietly and write in your journal.
2. Date each entry to track your progress over time.
3. Once a week, reread the previous days' entries to invite new insights.
4. Don't worry about doing it right. Your journal is unique!

24
JANUARY

LIFE-FORCE ENERGY

Life-force energy (what Taoists call *ch'i*) animates the physical body but also extends well beyond it. Life-force energy is the animating force of all-that-is, the vibratory nature of all phenomena.

25

ROTATING THE *TAN-T'IEN*

1. Stand with your feet shoulder-width apart; allow your head and spine to be vertically aligned.

2. Stack the palms of your hands one on top of the other, and place them lightly on your lower abdomen—a couple inches below your navel.

3. Imagine a shining orb—like a small sun—floating within the space of your lower *tan-t'ien*—the center of your pelvis.

4. Gently turn your hips and torso a few inches to the right, then back to center and then to the left. Repeat ten to fifteen times.

5. With your hips and torso centered, use your stacked palms to trace small circles on your abdomen, ten to fifteen times in each direction.

26
JANUARY

[The Sages of old] were careful
as someone crossing a frozen stream in winter.
Alert as if surrounded on all sides by the enemy.
Courteous as a guest.
Fluid as melting ice.
Whole as an uncarved block of wood.
Receptive as a valley.

TAO TE CHING, **CHAPTER 15**

27

JANUARY

UNCARVED BLOCK

Michelangelo's beautiful sculpture *David* began as a block of marble—creative potential not yet actualized.

Just so, your original primordial nature, itself formless, is pregnant with infinite creative potential. Contemplate this mystery.

28

JANUARY

MOMENTS OF CONTENTMENT

1. In the minutes before drifting off to sleep at night, reflect on the previous day—the things you did, the people you crossed paths with, and so on.

2. Recall moments that left you feeling inspired, amused, at ease, grateful, or content.

3. Let your attention linger a bit with these moments of contentment. Appreciate them deeply without trying to understand them. Let them bring a gentle smile to your face.

4. Drift off to sleep within this energy of appreciation.

29
JANUARY

—

FROM HAPPINESS

Explore the difference between actions, intentions, or goals that *emanate from* inner peace and happiness, and those that are motivated by a desire *to achieve* a peace or happiness that you believe is currently lacking.

30
JANUARY

—

THE MAGICAL "AHH"

Saying "ahh" is a simple yet profoundly effective way to release tension from the face, neck, and jaw.

As you say "ahh," your exhalation will naturally lengthen. You may also feel the soft palate—at the back of the roof of your mouth—release, creating a sense of spaciousness throughout your mouth.

As your face and neck and jaw relax, so will your shoulders, quite naturally.

Whenever you notice tension in your face or neck, close your eyes and say "ahh" two or three times, inviting the tensions to melt away.

31
JANUARY

RELEASING PRECONCEPTIONS

Saying "ahh" can also be a gesture of letting go of rigid preconceptions and beliefs about how things should or should not be.

Just for a moment, allow yourself to enter a space of utter and complete not-knowing.

FEBRUARY

1

FEBRUARY

GREETING THE SUN

1. Greet the sun as it rises at dawn.

2. Feel or imagine the energy of the rising sun flowing into your eyes and every pore of your skin—to energize you with its freshness and vitality.

3. Appreciate the importance of the sun to the body's physical survival. Express your gratitude in whatever way feels right.

4. Understand the playful irony of this ritual: Although the sun appears to rise and set, from a wider perspective it's actually the earth that turns toward and then away from it each day.

5. Appreciate the sun as a symbol of the eternal Sun of Awareness—the Light of Tao.

2
FEBRUARY
—
WONDER AND APPRECIATION

As you move through your day, endeavor to greet other human beings with the same wonder and appreciation as you greet a beautiful sunrise.

Does this come naturally or feel a bit awkward?

3
FEBRUARY
—

Therefore the Master
can act without doing anything
and teach without saying a word.
Things come her way and she does not stop them;
things leave and she lets them go.

TAO TE CHING, **CHAPTER 2**

4
FEBRUARY
—
CULTIVATION

A commitment to intelligent cultivation of the body and mind—via *ch'i-kung* (breath and movement practices) or sitting meditation—can be a beautiful thing.

Just remember: Your essential nature needs no cultivation!

5
FEBRUARY
—
ELEMENTAL

The elements that comprise your human body are the very same elements that comprise rivers, mountains, trees, clouds, and galaxies.

When the body dies, these elements simply get recycled, like autumn leaves becoming fertilizer for spring flowers.

6

FEBRUARY

STANDING MEDITATION #1

1. Stand with your feet shoulder-width apart and your toes pointing forward.

2. Let your hands hang loosely by your sides, with shoulders relaxed and a little bit of space between your fingers.

3. Imagine that your spine and entire body are suspended from the top of your head, like a puppet hanging on a string.

4. Relax your hips and belly and release your lower spine downward, as though you had a long tail that was resting on the floor between your feet.

5. Gaze forward and slightly downward; allow your chin to tuck slightly so your throat stays relaxed.

6. Breathe gently through your nose.

7. Simply stand still, in this position, for five minutes, noticing whatever physical sensations arise.

7
FEBRUARY
SONGBIRD

Sometimes birds sing to attract a mate or defend their territory. And sometimes they sing just for their own joy and celebration.

What kind of song will *you* be singing today?

8
FEBRUARY
WHICH BODY?

The cells of a human body replace themselves completely every seven to ten years. Once per decade, your body is utterly new.

Which of your bodies (if any) is the "real you"?

9

FEBRUARY

—

The Master puts herself last;
and finds herself in the place of authority.
She detaches herself from all things;
therefore she is united with all things.

TAO TE CHING, **CHAPTER 7**

10

FEBRUARY

—

MOON ON LAKE VISUALIZATION #1

1. Sit comfortably or lie down. Gently close your eyes.

2. Bring your attention to the center of your chest behind your sternum—the space of the middle *tan-t'ien*.

3. Imagine, within this space, a high-mountain lake, calm and pristine.

4. A full moon hovers above. And on the still surface of the lake, this full moon is reflected beautifully.

5. Imagine that you are sitting on the shore of this lake, gazing with appreciation at the moon's reflection—golden white, luminous.

6. Simply rest here, communing with the moon's reflection, for as long as you'd like.

11
FEBRUARY
PULSATION

Pulsation (cycles of increase and decrease) is a defining characteristic of the natural world—waxing and waning moon cycles, the inhale and exhale of the breath, an ocean tide rising and receding.

12
FEBRUARY
—
REFLECTED LIGHT

The light of the moon is reflected light; its source, the sun.

Just so, the light of the mind is reflected light; its source, Pure Awareness, the Light of Tao.

13
FEBRUARY
—
WALKING MEDITATION #1

1. Find a pleasant place to walk, indoors or out. A park or forest path is perfect, or a quiet room in your own home.

2. In a relaxed and gentle way, coordinate the rhythm of your breathing with your steps. For instance, inhale as you step your left foot and then exhale with the step of your right foot. Or inhale as you take two steps and then exhale with the next two steps.

3. Imagine with each step that you're kissing the earth through the soles of your feet. Appreciate this effortless intimacy with the ground. Smile gently. Enjoy yourself.

14
FEBRUARY

—

FREE AND EASY

It's in the spirit of "free and easy wandering" that Taoist Immortals move through their days. Ease and spontaneity, humor, and playfulness also abound.
  Why? Because they're not bound by rigid preconceptions about how things are or should be.

15
FEBRUARY

—

Both small and great things must equally possess form.
The mind cannot picture to itself a thing without form, nor
conceive a form of unlimited dimensions.

—CHUANG TZU (TRANSLATED BY HERBERT GILES)

16
FEBRUARY
—
DON'T BELIEVE EVERYTHING YOU THINK!

1. Just for fun, question the script that your mind presents to you rather than automatically accepting it as fact or divine fiat.

2. Imagine you're an actor who has been offered a role in a new movie. The director has sent you the script, and you can decide whether to accept the role.

3. Your mind's beliefs and assumptions are like the movie script. And you are the actor who can evaluate the script before agreeing to step into the role.

4. If your answer is *yes*, then inhabit the role with gusto. Have fun! And if your answer is *no*, then just set that script aside and trust that a better one will be on its way soon.

17

FEBRUARY

—

THOUGHTS

Like text and images on your phone, thoughts and images appear on the screen of your mind. Where do these thoughts come from? And where do they go when they disappear?

Look for the "answer" in your direct experience, not in thought.

18

FEBRUARY

—

WELL-BEING

It's wise to take good care of your body and mind. But true well-being lies in understanding that the source of *eternal* peace and joy is independent of all phenomena, including bodies and minds.

19
FEBRUARY

MEETING OF HEAVEN AND EARTH #1

1. Stand with your feet shoulder-width apart.

2. Press down gently through the soles of your feet, like a tree extending roots deep into the earth.

3. Lift your arms and rest the back of your hands gently on your forehead. From here, press your palms upward toward the sky, as far as is comfortable. Imagine you can touch the moon or your favorite non-Earth planet.

4. Reach down through your feet and upward through your palms simultaneously.

5. Imagine and *feel* your human body to be the meeting point of heaven/sky and earth. Be deeply nourished by both.

20
FEBRUARY

LEVELS OF SILENCE

Become aware of these three levels of silence:

- Silence of the ears: an absence of external sound

- Silence of the mind: an absence of internal chatter

- Silence of Being: the ever-present foundation of all sound and silence

21
FEBRUARY
—

Thirty spokes are joined together in a wheel,
but it is the center hole
that allows the wheel to function.
We mold clay into a pot,
but it is the emptiness inside
that makes the vessel useful.

TAO TE CHING, **CHAPTER 11**

22
FEBRUARY
—
MOVEMENT AND QUIETUDE

The heart, mind, and body are nourished by a harmonious balance of movement and quietude. As you move through your day, notice your tendencies and preferences around these two. Are there moments when they interpenetrate?

23

FEBRUARY

—

TUNING INTO WITNESS CONSCIOUSNESS

1. Choose an object in your environment to softly gaze at.

2. Shift your gaze to another object.

3. Notice that although the object has changed, the awareness that has witnessed the objects is the same.

4. Become interested in this witness consciousness that is *aware of* sights, sounds, tastes, smells, and tactile sensations, and is also *aware of* subtle objects such as thoughts and internal images, or *ch'i* sensations.

24

FEBRUARY

—

HIDE-AND-SEEK

When you close your eyes, the images of the external world disappear.

But do *you* disappear?

Now imagine being in a high-tech sensory deprivation tank, which could erase all sense perceptions as well as all thoughts and internal images. In such a scenario, who or what would remain?

25

FEBRUARY

—

EMPTY BOAT

If you're rowing a boat and an empty boat that accidentally became unmoored from its dock bangs into your boat, you don't feel too upset.

What if all boats are, *in reality*, empty boats?

26

FEBRUARY

—

TURNING THE LIGHT AROUND

Turning the light around means withdrawing the focus of Awareness from sense perceptions, physical sensations, and thoughts so that Awareness shines on itself alone, like a self-luminous sun. Here's how:

1. Close your eyes and become aware of the movement of your breath—the sounds and physical sensations associated with breathing.

2. Now, become aware of the Awareness that is noticing breath and physical sensations. Turn the Light of Awareness around to shine on itself alone.

3. Rest in and as this Awareness, which is the Light of Tao shining through your human body-mind.

27
FEBRUARY

—

If you open yourself to the Tao,
the Tao will eagerly welcome you.

TAO TE CHING, **CHAPTER 23**

28
FEBRUARY

—

HERE NOW

Ask yourself, What is here now if there's no problem to solve?

Can you find an internal "place" in which there is no sense of lack? Be open to the possibility that such a "place" does indeed exist.

29
FEBRUARY

MOON ON LAKE VISUALIZATION #2

1. Imagine, within the space of your middle *tan-t'ien*, a high-mountain lake, calm and pristine. And on the surface of this lake a full moon is reflected, beautifully.

2. As you sit on the shores of this lake, imagine the movement of your breath—the inhales and exhales—creating gentle ripples on the lake's surface. The breath ripples cause the moon's reflection also to ripple.

3. Feel and imagine these ripples, soaked in the radiance of moonlight, rippling out from this beautiful lake to every cell of your body.

4. After some time, allow the ripples to return to stillness, in the space of the middle *tan-t'ien*, your heart-center.

MARCH

1
MARCH
DEEPEST DESIRE

Ask yourself, What is my deepest desire?

Then, from a place of openness and genuine curiosity, listen for the answer.

Continue to ask the question until you feel an inner certainty and satisfaction.

2
MARCH
RECIPES FOR HAPPINESS

Your personal recipes for happiness are the strategies you've inherited from your parents, teachers, sports heroes, financial advisers, the media, or whomever. Which of these are *genuinely* effective in supporting lasting peace and happiness, and which are not? To explore this question:

1. Take out a piece of paper or open a blank document on your computer.

2. Complete the sentence *I will be happy if (or when)* . . .

3. Repeat this process a dozen times or more, repeatedly filling in the sentence *I will be happy if (or when)* . . .

4. Review what you've written and ask yourself, Which of these strategies have been successful, and which have not? Be honest!

3
MARCH
—

POSITIONLESS

Chuang Tzu's freedom from societal dictates arose from an alignment with his inner knowing, his true nature.

He wasn't inhabiting the position of a victim, a rebel, or a tyrant. He was instead flowing with the positionless wisdom of the Tao.

4
MARCH
—

It is all right to abandon compass and square
if you are a mirror held up to real shapes.

—**LU JI** (TRANSLATED BY BARNSTONE/PING IN *THE ART OF WRITING: TEACHINGS OF THE CHINESE MASTERS*)

5
MARCH

PATH AND DESTINATION

The Tao is a way—a path. It's also the origin of all phenomena and the destination of Taoist practice. How can Tao simultaneously be origin, path, and destination?

Taoism is a nondual path, which means that at each step there is the opportunity to notice that you're already at the destination!

6
MARCH

THE YIN-YANG SYMBOL

Contemplate the wisdom of the Taoist yin-yang symbol, which represents duality emerging from the unity of Tao and how pairs of opposites contain each other.

The black and white sides of the symbol illustrate yin and yang: the primordial feminine and masculine energies. The dance of yin and yang—their movement within the field of time and space—gives birth to all the objects/events of the universe.

The black side holds a seed of white, and the white side a seed of black. Like the two sides of a coin, pairs of opposites are always interdependent and mutually arising.

By understanding the interdependence of pairs of opposites, a Taoist practitioner avoids unnecessary suffering.

7

MARCH

PATIENCE

Although you can plant seeds and water them, you can't pull the young sprouts to make them grow faster.

Each thing in the natural world unfolds in its own time.

8
MARCH

Those who stand on tiptoes
do not stand firmly.
Those who rush ahead
don't get very far.
Those who try to outshine others
dim their own light.

TAO TE CHING, **CHAPTER 24**

9
MARCH

MIRROR AND IMAGE

1. Stand in front of a mirror.

2. Observe the shapes and colors of the objects (including your own human body) reflected in the mirror. See how you can identify visual boundaries between the objects; each is different from the other.

3. Place your fingertip on the mirror, and close your eyes. Slowly move your fingertip across the mirror. Can you feel any tactile distinctions as you move your finger from place to place?

4. Keeping your finger on the mirror, open your eyes again. Understand that the substance, the shared essence, of all reflections is the mirror.

5. Just so, all phenomena share a single essence, are of "one taste"—Pure Awareness, the Light of Tao.

10
MARCH

ONE AND MANY

One (Tao) gives birth to two (*yin-ch'i* and *yang-ch'i*),
    which create the five elements,
    which generate the ten thousand things:
    all the objects/events of our worldly existence.

11
MARCH

—

Look at this window: it is nothing but a hole in the wall, but because of it the whole room is full of light. So, when the faculties are empty, the heart is full of light.

—CHUANG TZU (TRANSLATED BY THOMAS MERTON, *THE WAY OF CHUANG TZU*)

12
MARCH
RIVERS OF CH'I

Acupuncture meridians are like rivers of life-force energy. If these rivers become blocked or stagnant, disease can emerge. When they flow freely, with balance and measured fullness, then the body-mind is healthy.

13
MARCH
TAPPING THE ARM MERIDIANS

1. Stand with your feet hip-width apart.

2. Use the palm of your right hand to tap down the inner edge of your left arm, beginning from the inner left shoulder.

3. Once you've reached your left palm (tapping it with your right palm), continue tapping up the outer edge of your left arm to the back of your left shoulder.

4. Repeat on the other side, using your left palm to tap down the inner edge and up the outer edge of your right arm/hand.

5. Move back and forth, from side to side, five to eight times.

6. To conclude the practice, run your palms smoothly (rather than tapping) along the same course, once or twice.

MARCH

MOUNTAIN

Mountains exude unshakable stability, natural dignity, and a vast far-reaching view. Can you be strong and stable like a mountain or access a place within yourself that effortlessly emanates similar qualities?

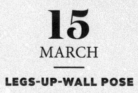

MARCH

LEGS-UP-WALL POSE

To help release tension and rejuvenate your entire body:

1. Sit on the floor with your hips six to ten inches away from a wall.

2. Release your torso to the floor as you swing your legs up (at an angle) against the wall.

3. Support your head with a pillow, if you'd like, or just let it rest directly on the floor.

4. Rest your arms on the floor near your torso, or out from your shoulders, or with palms on your belly, or fingers interlaced behind your head.

5. Relax deeply in this position for ten to fifteen minutes.

6. When you're ready, slide your feet halfway down the wall and gently roll onto your side. After a couple of minutes, push slowly up to sitting.

16
MARCH
DOING LESS

Consider the possibility that positive results can come from doing less rather than more. Experiment with applying this to some aspect of your life.

17
MARCH

FENG-SHUI

Balancing the flow of life-force energy through the body's meridians is the realm of acupuncture. Balancing the flow of life-force energy through a living space or external environment is the realm of *feng-shui*.

18
MARCH

BRING BALANCE TO YOUR LIVING SPACE

Experiment with the principles of *feng-shui*, either formally, by using a text-book as your guide to follow established principles, or more intuitively.

The basic idea is to create a harmonious flow of life-force energy within your living environment, which supports a sense of comfort and ease for all who dwell or visit there.

The first step is to notice energetic imbalances—places of harsh or stagnant *ch'i*—and then remedy these imbalances by rearranging furniture or adding classic *feng-shui* elements such as mirrors, water fountains, or pleasant plants, flowers, or artwork.

19
MARCH

—

All things end in the Tao
just as the small streams and the largest rivers
flow through valleys to the sea.

TAO TE CHING, **CHAPTER 32**

20
MARCH

—

WHAT THE CREEK SAYS

Sit on the bank of a creek or river.

Listen to its song—all the various sounds that it makes. Do this with your eyes open and then with your eyes gently closed.

Feel as though you're merging with the sound of the flowing water, dissolving into the sound fully.

Contemplate the creek's movement, and the relative stillness of your body, sitting on its banks.

And yet there are rivers of blood flowing through the veins and arteries of your body. And rivers of breath moving into and out of your lungs.

Is there such a thing as absolute stillness? If so, what is its source?

21
MARCH
—
ANIMAL FRIENDS

Notice which nonhuman animals you resonate most deeply with or the ones that most inspire you. What is it about them that you so appreciate? What is it that leaves you feeling delighted and amazed?

22
MARCH
—
FRUITFUL IMITATION

1. Just for fun, play with imitating the movement of animals, particularly the ones that most inspire you.

2. Watch closely how they move, in water, over land, or through the sky. Notice how they eat, sleep, and interact with other members of their species. Notice how they hide, fight, and/or retreat when confronted with danger. Notice their mating rituals, what they do to impress a potential mate. Notice how they relax and play.

3. See if you can do the same, and notice how you feel.

4. This is how many *ch'i-kung* forms were created.

5. Each animal has its own wisdom and power, which you can discover by embodying its movements.

23
MARCH

DEEP ROOTS

Trees with deep roots can maintain stability even in the face of high winds.
    Can you do the same?
    Can you find your physical roots, the legs and lower *tan-t'ien*?
    Can you find an even deeper grounding in Pure Awareness—the Light of Tao?

24
MARCH

COMMUNING WITH A TREE

1. Lean your back against the trunk of a tree. Say *hello*.

2. Close your eyes to deeply feel this sweet connection with your tree friend.

3. Imagine roots growing down from the soles of your feet to intermingle with the roots of the tree.

4. Imagine your spine merging with the tree trunk, and notice how it feels to draw sap upward from roots along the centerline.

5. Imagine how it feels for this sap to nourish the growth of branches and leaves—the tree's version of arms lifted skyward.

6. Deeply receive the blessings of the tree, its sharing of life-force energy.

7. Say *thank you* before continuing on your way.

25
MARCH

—

SYMBIOSIS

What a beautiful symbiosis human beings have with trees! What humans exhale (carbon dioxide), the trees absorb through their leaves. And what trees release into the environment (oxygen), humans gratefully receive with each inhale.

26
MARCH

—

The Tao is nameless and unchanging.
Although it appears insignificant,
nothing in the world can contain it.

TAO TE CHING, **CHAPTER 32**

27
MARCH

QUERY

The eternal Tao, your essential nature, is ineffable.
    What does this mean? Ask yourself:
    Does your innermost essence have a shape, size, or color?
    Can it be enhanced or degraded?
    Does it have a boundary?
    Was it born?
    Can it die?

28
MARCH

EXPANDING THE SENSE OF SELF

1. Imagine your skin is the skin of a bubble. Inside the bubble are your body's bones and organs; outside is the so-called external world.

2. Is it your habit to consider the inside of the skin bubble as "me" and the outside as "not-me"?

3. The *ch'i* that animates your body's organs is not bound by the skin. It can expand outward.

4. Imagine expanding the bubble skin outward, beyond your physical skin. Expand it to encompass your entire house or apartment and then the whole city, state, and continent.

5. Expand the bubble to encompass the planet Earth, the Milky Way galaxy, and the entire cosmos.

6. Ask yourself, Who or what is this "me" that contains the entire cosmos?

29
MARCH
——
INSIDE OUT

At the level of your direct experience:

Is Awareness in your physical body?

Or does your body—experienced as physical sensations, visual perceptions, and thoughts—appear within Awareness?

30
MARCH

ROCK DIVINATION

1. Next time you go on a hike or walk, be on the lookout for a medium-size rock, one that calls to you.

2. Formulate a question that currently feels important to you, and write it down in your journal or on your computer or phone.

3. Place the rock in front of you, and gaze softly at one of its (four or five or six) sides, as though gazing at a beautiful painting.

4. Write down what you see (i.e., what the various shapes, colors, and textures evoke in your mind's eye). Don't think too much about it; just free-associate.

5. Repeat this process for the other "sides" of the rock.

6. Reread your question and journal on the "answers" received from your rock friend.

31
MARCH

—

CRYSTALLINE WHISPER

Add a favorite crystal or gemstone to your living environment. Do you experience this member of the mineral kingdom as a "living being"? How do you communicate with each other?

APRIL

1
APRIL
—
RELAXED ALERTNESS

In meditation, you can become deeply relaxed without falling asleep and maintain a bright alertness without becoming tense or hyper. This is the relaxed alertness of the Taoist sage.

In meditation, great ease and great wakefulness live together happily.

2
APRIL
—
ABDOMINAL BREATHING

1. Lie down on your back, either on the floor or on your bed. Hinge your knees to allow the soles of your feet to rest flat on the floor or bed.

2. Place the palms of your hands gently on your lower belly, near or slightly below the navel.

3. Smile gently and say "ahh" a couple times with the exhalation to fully relax your face, neck, and jaw.

4. Inhale deeply enough that you can feel your abdomen lifting upward into your palms.

5. As you exhale, notice your belly naturally relaxing back toward the floor or bed.

6. Repeat ten to fifteen times, allowing your abdomen to rise and fall with the breathing cycle.

3
APRIL

—

Love the whole world as if it were your self;
then you will truly care for all things.

TAO TE CHING, **CHAPTER 13**

4
APRIL

THREE TREASURES

Explore and cherish the Three Treasures of Inner Alchemy:

* *Ching* (also spelled: *jing*): creative energy

* *Ch'i* (also spelled: *qi*): life-force energy

* *Shen:* spiritual energy

  How do you experience each of these?

5
APRIL

NOTICING THE SPACE BETWEEN

Here's a figure-ground reversal that can be fun to play with:

1. Every now and again, shift your visual focus away from objects and toward the *space between* objects. For instance, instead of noticing the shape and color of a chair and end table, notice the space *between* and *around* these objects.

2. Let the space become more "real" than the objects, and notice how this perceptual shift transforms your experience.

3. Once you're comfortable noticing the space between external objects, try the same thing with your thoughts, which are more subtle "objects."

4. Can you notice the silent gaps *between* the words and sentences of your mind's internal chatter? What happens when you linger and rest in these silent spaces?

6
APRIL
—

NATURALLY FLUID AND BRIGHT

If you devote some time each day to sitting quietly, your capacity to think clearly will be enhanced. Your mind will regain its natural state of being fluid and energetic, buoyant and pliable, bright as a diamond.

7
APRIL

RELATIVE IMPORTANCE

If you were to lose a little finger, it would be painful, but your body would likely survive.

If the sun were to go supernova and disappear from the sky, would your body survive this more "distant" injury?

Now ask yourself, Which is more genuinely "me," my little finger or the sun?

8
APRIL

FEEDING THE FIVE ORGANS

According to the five-element theory of Chinese medicine, each organ system is associated with a specific color. You can "feed" your organs by offering them their favorite color of light. Here's how:

1. With an exhale, imagine sending beautiful emerald-green light to your liver. Allow this light to envelop and soak deeply into the cells of your liver. Feel your liver receiving this gift, with gratitude.

2. In the same way, send beautiful ruby-red light to your heart, golden light to your spleen, white light to your lungs, and deep-blue or purple light to your kidneys.

9
APRIL
—

The greatest virtue you can have comes from following only the Tao.

TAO TE CHING, **CHAPTER 21**

10
APRIL
—
DREAMLIKE

Consider this beloved nursery rhyme as whispered wisdom from the Taoist Immortals:

Row, row, row your boat
gently down the stream.

>>>

Merrily, merrily, merrily, merrily
life is but a dream.
Can you see the dreamlike qualities of your life?

11
APRIL

WALKING MEDITATION #2

1. Find a pleasant place to walk, indoors or out.

2. In a relaxed way, coordinate the rhythm of your breathing with your steps. For instance, inhale as you step your left foot and then exhale with the step of your right foot. Or inhale as you take two steps and then exhale with the next two steps.

3. Add a gentle swinging of your arms and hands side to side at the level of your lower *tan-t'ien*, with your palms facing the ground and your fingers relaxed.

4. As you step with your left foot, swing your hands gently to the left. As you step with your right foot, swing your hands gently to the right.

12
APRIL
RESPONSE-ABILITY

Reactivity is action emerging from the mistaken belief in a separate self—a personal limited "me" that is separate from all else.

True *response-ability* (the capacity to respond authentically and effectively with wisdom and compassion) arises from the understanding that whatever is happening is "nothing personal."

13
APRIL
ROSE-COLORED GLASSES

If you wear rose-tinted sunglasses, then everything, even the lily-white snow, appears rose-colored.

Letting go of habitual beliefs and preconceptions is like taking off the rose-colored glasses and once again seeing things clearly, nakedly, as they really are.

14
APRIL

LEG THREE LI

Perhaps the most famous of all acupuncture points is Stomach 36, also known as "Leg Three Li." A Chinese *li* is a distance equal to about one-third mile.

According to legend, activating the Leg Three Li point will energize an exhausted traveler enough to allow them to walk another three li.

Leg Three Li is located three *cun*—the width of your four fingers (minus the thumb)—below your kneecap, about an inch outside of the bony ridge of your shinbone.

Use the end of one of your fingers to massage this point for thirty seconds to three minutes, as often as you'd like, throughout the day.

15
APRIL

—

To age with the sun and moon and be renewed by spring and summer, to conserve the seeds of growth in autumn and winter and to be nourished by the eternal breath of the Tao, these are the goals of the Taoist alchemists, the masters of the arts of health, longevity, and immortality.

—EVA WONG, *HARMONIZING YIN AND YANG*

16
APRIL

—

PRECIOUS HUMAN BODY

Respect and care for your precious human body, without losing sight of its ephemeral nature.

Because of the impermanence—the perpetual transformation—of its cells, both disease and healing are possible.

17
APRIL

EARTH NOURISHMENT

Your ancestors walked barefoot and slept directly on the ground much more than you likely do today. Their bodies were nourished directly by the resonance—the electromagnetic heartbeat—of the earth.

Over time, human beings have spent less time outdoors, so less time in direct contact with the earth. But you can regain the benefits of a more intimate connection.

How? By standing, walking barefoot, or lying down in the grass to connect more directly with earth energy.

Any opportunity for your physical body to directly contact the ground, in a safe and relaxed way, is a good thing!

18
APRIL

ENERGY IN MOTION

Consider emotions to be energy in motion: e-motion.

In Chinese medicine, each emotion corresponds to a specific organ. Stagnant *ch'i* can manifest as anger, fear, grief, pensiveness, or anxiety that becomes chronic. Balanced and free-flowing *ch'i* supports kindness, courage, generosity, joy, and equanimity.

19
APRIL

RESONANCE

When your body, mind, and heart become balanced and harmonious, your capacity for empathy will naturally expand. Through the resonance of an expanded *ch'i* field and/or the operation of mirror neurons, you're able to intuit how others are feeling.

20
APRIL

HOW TO MAKE CHAGA TEA

Mushrooms (friends from the fungi kingdom) can be a nourishing addition to your diet. Shiitake, maitake, portobello, and lion's mane are delicious sautéed or baked. Reishi, agarikon, cordyceps, and turkey tail are staples of Chinese herbal medicine. And chaga makes a delicious tea!

1. Purchase dried chaga chunks.

2. Grind them in a coffee grinder.

3. Place some of the ground chaga with water in a pot.

4. Bring to a boil; then reduce the heat and cover.

5. Add a piece of whole vanilla bean and simmer for thirty to forty-five minutes.

6. Strain the liquid into a cup.

7. Sweeten with pure maple syrup and, if you'd like, add a splash of almond milk or half-and-half.

Enjoy!

21
APRIL

When the Tao is forgotten, there is righteousness.
When righteousness is forgotten, there is morality.
When morality is forgotten, there is the law.
The law is the husk of faith,
and [blind] trust is the beginning of chaos.

TAO TE CHING, **CHAPTER 38**

22
APRIL

SOFT BELLY

A newborn's belly is naturally soft. And an adult belly full of *ch'i*—life-force energy—can maintain a similar softness: buoyant and relaxed. Strength in your deeper core muscles eliminates the need for six-pack abs.

23
APRIL

INCUBATING THE GOOSE EGG

1. Sit upright in a padded chair or cross-legged on a cushion.

2. Rub the palms of your hands together until they're warm.

3. Slip one of your hands, with the palm facing upward, between your legs and all the way under the base of your torso, so you're sitting right on top of your palm, like a goose sitting on an egg.

4. Feel and/or imagine the *ch'i* from your palm flowing upward as nourishment for your pelvic floor, lower *tan-t'ien*, and reproductive organs. Continue for two to three minutes.

5. To complete the practice, rest your palms on top of your thighs; bring your focus to your heart-center and then to the space in the center of your head. Feel the connection between the three *tan-t'iens*.

24
APRIL

ALREADY AWAKE

Awareness is already awake, without your help.
   Already perfect, it requires no enhancement.
   And nothing you could do could possibly destroy it.
   So . . . relax!

25
APRIL

IN THE ZONE

Athletes, musicians, and artists who are "in the zone" function with optimal ease and efficiency, which opens the door to creative genius. In Taoism this is known as *wu-wei*.

26
APRIL

STANDING MEDITATION #2

1. Stand with your feet shoulder-width apart and your toes pointing forward.

2. As though you were hugging a big balloon, lift your arms up in front of your torso in a circular shape with your palms facing the center of your chest and the tips of your fingers four to six inches apart.

3. Keep your head and spine vertically aligned, like a puppet hanging on a string, and allow your hips and tailbone to relax downward.

4. Gaze forward and slightly downward; tuck your chin a bit so your throat stays relaxed.

5. Breathe gently through your nose.

6. Stand still in this position for five minutes, noticing whatever physical sensations arise.

27
APRIL

The Tao hides in the unnamed,
Yet it alone nourishes and completes all things.

TAO TE CHING, **CHAPTER 41**

28
APRIL

ANTICS OF THE IMMORTALS

Be delighted and inspired by tales of the Immortals:

- *Immortal Sisters* by Thomas Cleary
- *Tales of Taoist Immortals* by Eva Wong
- *Legends of the Mahasiddhas* by Keith Dowman

29
APRIL

BATHING THE SENSE ORGANS

1. Rub the palms of your hands together for fifteen to twenty seconds.

2. Cup your newly energized palms over your closed eyes.

3. As you inhale, imagine *ch'i* from your hands being drawn gently into your eyes and then from your eyes down to your liver.

4. As you exhale, imagine liver *ch'i* flowing like a healing stream up into your eyes. Repeat for five to ten breaths.

5. Do the same thing with your ears and kidneys: Cup your hands over your ears; then breathe *ch'i* from your palms to your ears to your kidneys on the inhale and your kidneys to your ears on the exhale.

6. This practice is perfect for giving your eyes and ears a break from your phone or computer screen!

30
APRIL

WISE CONSUMPTION

In the same way that you attend mindfully to the food that you eat, be aware of your heart-mind's "diet"—the media, relationships, events, and conversations that you consume throughout the day. Endeavor to consume what's nourishing rather than what's toxic.

MAY

1

MAY

MYSTERY

The Tao is ineffable, ever-present, and eternal.
It is also what is most intimate, closer than close, essential, indestructible.
Appreciate this mystery of the ineffable Tao.

2

MAY

The tao that can be described
is not the eternal Tao.
The name that can be spoken
is not the eternal Name.

TAO TE CHING, **CHAPTER 1**

3
MAY

ABDOMINAL MASSAGE

It's best to do this practice with an empty stomach and wearing comfortable clothes:

1. Lie down on the floor, faceup, with your knees hinged and feet resting flat, about hip-distance apart. If you'd like, place a pillow under your head.

2. Rub the palms of your hands together for fifteen to twenty seconds.

3. Using your energized palms, gently stroke downward from the bottom of your ribs to your lower abdomen, moving side to side.

4. Stack your palms one on top of the other, and use your stacked palms to massage your belly in a circular motion, ten times in one direction and then ten times in the opposite direction.

5. Like a gentle mist, direct smile-energy into your deep belly.

4
MAY

FOSSILS

Don't hold on to philosophies (even the *Tao Te Ching*) too tightly. They are just approximations, fingers pointing to the moon, maps outlining a territory.

Conceptual descriptions of the Tao are like fossils that represent but can never replace the living organism.

5
MAY

VORTEX

Consider a vortex within a stream, a spiraling pattern of water. It defines a unique shape that is never actually separate from the totality of stream water.

Consider human body-minds as being something similar.

6
MAY

TAPPING THE LEG MERIDIANS

1. Stand or sit on a chair with your feet hip-width apart.

2. Using the palms of your hands (both at the same time), tap down the outer edge of the corresponding legs, beginning from your outer hips and ending at your little toes.

3. Once you've reached your little toes (or as far as you can reach), continue tapping up the inner edge of your feet and legs, from your big toes to the front-inner edge of your hips.

4. Repeat five to eight times.

5. To conclude the practice, run your palms smoothly (rather than tapping) along the same course once or twice.

7
MAY
—

TRANSPORT

Walk or bike instead of driving whenever you can.

Enjoy the new strength in your hips and legs, the energy in your core, and the nice massage the earth offers the soles of your feet.

8
MAY
—

For those who practice not-doing,
everything will fall into place.

TAO TE CHING, **CHAPTER 3**

9
MAY
—
KEEPING THE ONE

1. Sit comfortably, and gently close your eyes.

2. Take a few deep, slow breaths, noticing how the breath feels in your body.

3. Relax that intentional focus on the breath, allowing it to continue in its own natural rhythm.

4. Notice that all physical sensations (including those related to breathing), as well as sounds, scents, thoughts, and internal images, appear within your Awareness, like waves rising and falling on the surface of the ocean.

5. Rather than being interested in the thoughts, perceptions, or sensations, just let them come and go, as *you*—unchanging Awareness, the Light of Tao—remain.

6. Aside from this simple, effortless resting as Awareness, do nothing.

10
MAY

UNBOUNDED WHOLENESS

There are many varieties of gold ornaments: bracelets, rings, necklaces. But their shared substance is gold. Many ornaments, one gold.

Just so, the ten thousand things (all the objects/events of the cosmos) are simply ornaments of the Tao.

11
MAY

WHITE SKELETON MEDITATION

1. Sit comfortably or lie down.

2. Gently close your eyes and say "ahh" a couple times to help relax your face, neck, and jaw.

3. Feel and/or imagine your skeleton, the structural scaffolding of your physical body.

4. Imagine the bones of your skeleton in as much detail as you can. Imagine them being pure white in color.

5. Imagine these pure white bones beginning to shine brightly and then transforming into pure white light, so your bones are now made of white light.

6. Imagine and feel these luminous bones dissolving completely into the space around them.

7. What supports your physical body is a shimmering field of pure white light.

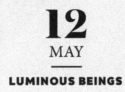

12
MAY
LUMINOUS BEINGS

Who could argue that Yoda (Luke Skywalker's mentor in *Star Wars*) is anything but a Taoist sage?

"Luminous beings are we, not this crude matter. You must feel the Force around you; here, between you, me, the tree, the rock, everywhere, yes."

13
MAY

MATCHA

A favorite drink among *ch'i-kung* and meditation practitioners is matcha. What makes it so excellent? It's the presence of L-theanine, an amino acid that stimulates the production of alpha waves in the brain, which supports a state of relaxed alertness.

14
MAY

The mind of the Sage, being in repose, becomes the mirror of the universe, the speculum of all creation.

—CHUANG TZU (TRANSLATED BY HERBERT GILES)

15
MAY

SOOTHING THE NERVOUS SYSTEM

1. Sit comfortably or lie down.

2. Gently close your eyes.

3. Cup the base of your skull, where your head meets your neck, with one of your palms, as though cradling a newborn.

4. Allow the weight of your head to release into the support of your hand.

5. Rest your other palm gently on your forehead.

6. Maintain this gentle nourishing contact between your palms and your head (front and back) while keeping your arms and shoulders as relaxed as possible.

7. Feel into the space between your two palms—the center of your skull. Send a gentle smile into that space.

16
MAY
—

TREASURE HUNT

You'll never find an object that exists *sui generis*—wholly independent of its causes and conditions, its parts, and/or your perceptions and thoughts about it.

But just because things don't exist as independent entities doesn't mean that they are nothing. Rather, their no-thing-ness reveals ineffable radiance.

17
MAY
—

WHICH IS MOST RELIABLE?

To explore the validity of your beliefs, understand the difference between direct experience, inference, and hearsay.

You can *directly experience* the shape, color, and scent of a flower. *Inference* is a conclusion reached by logical reasoning. And *hearsay* is what someone else says.

18
MAY

EXTENDING THE EXHALATION

1. Sit comfortably, either in a chair or on a cushion on the floor.

2. Bring your attention to the movement of your breath, its inhalations and exhalations. Notice the qualities of your breath: Is it deep or shallow? Is it smooth or choppy? Just notice, without judgment or mental commentary.

3. Begin to gently lengthen your exhalations so they're a bit longer than the inhalations. For instance, if your inhale takes five seconds (counted to yourself), allow your exhale to extend to eight seconds.

4. If possible, breathe through your nose for the entire breathing cycle.

5. Repeat for ten rounds of breath, and notice how you feel.

19
MAY

FUZZY LOGIC

Can you find a rigid boundary between inside and outside?

Your body's skin is semipermeable. Your breath comes in and out. And your mind is continuously influenced by sights and sounds of the so-called external world.

20
MAY

The knowledge and skills you have achieved are meant to be forgotten so you can float comfortably in emptiness, without obstruction.

—BRUCE LEE

21

MAY

FRUITFUL FORGETTING

Mastery of a martial arts or *ch'i-kung* form begins with learning skills and then being able to forget them, trusting that they will appear exactly when you need them.

Cultivate this balance between learning and unlearning.

22

MAY

PAINTING THE ROOM

1. Sit or stand with your feet shoulder-width apart.

2. Rest your palms on the front of your thighs.

3. With an inhale, float your arms and hands upward in front of your torso until they reach the level of your heart, keeping them shoulder-width apart with elbows gently hinged.

4. As you exhale, float them back to their starting point, resting lightly on your thighs.

5. Keep your hands and fingers relaxed and fluid—as though they were soft paintbrushes.

6. Imagine your fingers—the flexible bristles of the two brushes—"painting" the walls of the room with *ch'i* that is flowing through the tips of your fingers. Continue for one to two minutes.

23
MAY

WEATHER PATTERNS

Clouds can be fluffy white or ferociously lightning filled—Mother Nature in her peaceful and wrathful moods. But the sky doesn't have a preference, nor is it essentially altered in any way by this or that weather pattern.

You are the sky.

24
MAY

TAPPING THE KIDNEYS

1. Stand with your feet shoulder-width apart.

2. Keep your head and spine vertically aligned and your hips relaxed.

3. Curl your fingers into loose fists.

4. Gently rotate your head, torso, and hips side to side, allowing your arms to swing freely as you do so.

5. As you rotate to the right, let your right fist tap your mid-back at the level of your kidneys. As you rotate to the left, let your left fist tap your mid-back.

6. As you tap your kidneys, send the energy of a smile, as though you were saying, "Hello, my precious kidneys, and thank you!"

7. Continue for thirty to sixty seconds, or longer if you'd like.

25
MAY

ADAPTABILITY

Bristlecone pine trees can live five thousand years! This longevity results from harsh living conditions (mountain altitudes, cold temperatures, and high winds), which combine to create super-dense wood that's resistant to insects, fungi, and rot.

Can you also transform adversity into something positive?

26

MAY

SCALP AND EAR MASSAGE

1. Rub the palms of your hands together for fifteen to twenty seconds.

2. If you're wearing glasses, remove them.

3. Use your fingertips and/or nails to vigorously massage your scalp, from front to back. Begin at the centerline of your head (forehead to the base of your skull) and move progressively closer to your ears.

4. Use the ends of your fingers to tap your skull in the same pattern, front to back.

5. "Comb" your hair with your fingers and smooth it using the palms of your hands.

6. Massage your ears, gently squeezing, tugging, and folding the lobe and other parts of the external ear.

27
MAY

—

Can you focus your life-breath until you become supple as a newborn child?

TAO TE CHING, **CHAPTER 10**

28
MAY

—

LAO TZU IN HOLLYWOOD

Enjoy a film or TV series with Taoist themes:

- *Kung Fu* (with David Carradine)
- *Crouching Tiger, Hidden Dragon*
- *Enter the Dragon*
- *Hero* (with Jet Li)
- *Why Has Bodhi-Dharma Left for the East?*

- *Star Wars*
- *Groundhog Day*
- *Forrest Gump*
- *Avatar*

29
MAY

IT'S ALL RELATIVE

1. Collect three sticks of different lengths.

2. Place them side by side on the floor or a table; identify the medium-size stick.

3. Remove the longest stick, and put it to the side, out of sight.

4. Notice that what used to be the "medium-size stick" is now (among the two remaining) the longest stick.

5. Bring all three sticks back into view.

6. Remove the shortest stick, and put it to the side, out of sight.

7. Notice that what used to be the "medium-size stick" is now (among the two remaining) the shortest stick.

8. Ask yourself, What is the actual truth of this stick? Is it medium-size, long, or short?

30
MAY

REMEDY

Next time you feel like you've "gotten the short stick" in a particular situation, recall the relativity of dimension and (as Chuang Tzu would) have a good laugh.

31
MAY

INNER SMILE #2

1. Find a quiet place to sit or lie down.

2. Rest your attention lightly at the center of your forehead; then let it drift back to the center of your skull.

3. Smile gently with your entire being as well as your mouth. Allow your eyes to become smiling eyes.

4. With these smiling eyes, gaze inwardly to your liver. Imagine smile-energy gently enveloping this organ, as though giving a warm hug to a friend you haven't seen for a long while.

5. In the same way, smile inwardly to your heart, spleen, lungs, and kidneys—then back to your liver.

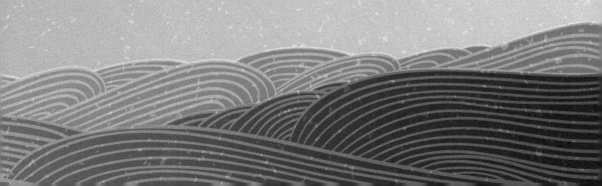

JUNE

1
JUNE

EYE AND I

Your human eye cannot directly see itself.

Just so, invisible Awareness (which is aware of these words right now) can never see itself as an object, though this "I" knows itself directly, by effortlessly *being* itself.

2
JUNE

Whoever knows contentment will be at peace forever.

TAO TE CHING, **CHAPTER 46**

3
JUNE

FLAVORS OF IMMORTALITY

In Taoism, the word *immortality* can mean:

- Cultivating physical longevity via *ch'i-kung* practice, dietary strategies, and herbal formulas.

- Becoming a Taoist wizard with seemingly miraculous, magical powers.

- Being a realized sage—a spiritual master—who is in continuous alignment with the Tao.

Which of these "flavors" of immortality interests you most? Why?

Are you most enthused about extending the life of your physical body, achieving extraordinary powers, or discovering your essential nature as the Light of Tao?

There is no right or wrong answer, but it's useful to be clear about your motivation.

4
JUNE

CENTERING

When you bring the palms of your hands together in front of your chest, your attention and subtle energy are drawn to the centerline, at the level of the heart. This is the esoteric meaning of the prayer position.

5
JUNE

ABOUT-FACE

If you're in the habit of wearing facial makeup, then abstain for a few days. And if this isn't your habit, then wear makeup for a while.

Notice how these non-habitual actions make you feel: fearful, vulnerable, silly, naked, adventurous, exhilarated?

6
JUNE

GOLDEN ELIXIR

1. Sit comfortably, and gently close your eyes.

2. Use your tongue to massage your gums, both their inner and outer edges.

3. As you do this, saliva will begin to gather in your mouth. Soon, you'll have a nice pool of this "golden elixir."

4. "Chew" the saliva—swish it around and gently tap your teeth, as though you were chewing food.

5. Once you've chewed the saliva for about ten seconds, swallow it, with the clear intention to send the saliva to your lower *tan-t'ien*, as fuel for that energetic space.

6. Of course, the saliva won't *actually* go to your lower abdomen, but you can direct its energetic essence there.

7
JUNE

UNCONTRIVED WISDOM

Every living being (plant, mineral, or animal) already contains the best version of itself. Like a blueprint for optimal unfolding, this uncontrived wisdom is inherent and requires no interference.

Can you trust that the same is true for you as well?

8
JUNE

Those who know others are intelligent;
those who know themselves are truly wise.
Those who master others are strong;
those who master themselves have true power.

TAO TE CHING, **CHAPTER 33**

9
JUNE
—
LION'S ROAR

1. Stand or sit with your spine upright and eyes softly open.

2. Clench your fists tightly, and place them on either side of your waist, drawing your elbows and shoulders back to widen your chest.

3. Take a long, slow inhalation.

4. With the exhalation, stick your tongue out as far as it will go, open your eyes extra wide, and fully extend your arms, hands, and fingers out in front of your torso, like a lion extending sharp claws.

5. As you extend your tongue and claw fingers, make an aspirant sound with the breath—the lion's "roar."

6. Repeat this three to five times, letting the lion's roar emanate from your heart-center in a gesture of openhearted ferocity.

10
JUNE

REFLECTIONS

A single full moon can be reflected upon the surface of many ponds.

Just so, the eternal Light of Tao (nondual Pure Awareness) is reflected through a multitude of human heart-minds.

11
JUNE

HONORING

With each meal, give thanks to the plants and animals that sacrificed their lives to support the life of your human body.

Then be curious about how you might *embody* the most sublime qualities of those beings to honor their blessing, their benediction, their selfless offering.

12
JUNE

STANDING MEDITATION #3

1. Stand with your feet shoulder-width apart and your toes pointing forward.

2. Float your arms up in front of your abdomen in a circular shape with your palms facing your lower *tan-t'ien* (a couple inches below your navel) and the tips of your fingers four to six inches apart.

3. Keep your head and spine vertically aligned, like a puppet hanging on a string, and allow your hips and tailbone to relax downward.

4. Gaze forward and slightly downward. Tuck your chin a bit so your throat stays relaxed.

5. Breathe gently through your nose.

6. Simply stand still in this position for five minutes, noticing whatever physical sensations arise.

13
JUNE

HELP ALONG THE WAY

Welcome the presence of a teacher, a practice partner, and/or a spiritual community for valuable guidance and camaraderie.

Although it may at times be necessary to walk the path alone, it's always nice to have friends.

14
JUNE

To attain perfect happiness and harmony in life, [Chuang Tzu] says, you need not become a sage; it is sufficient to free your mind and flow along smoothly with the course of Tao.

—LIVIA KOHN, *CHUANG-TZU: THE TAO OF PERFECT HAPPINESS*

15
JUNE

On the soles of your feet is an acupuncture point called "Bubbling Spring," which is a great one to massage. Here's how:

1. Take off your shoes and, if you'd like, your socks, too.

2. Sit in a chair or couch—someplace where you can comfortably rest one ankle over the opposite knee.

3. Use the ends of your thumbs to firmly massage the bottom of your foot, particularly in the center near the base of your big toe, second toe, and third toe.

4. Continue for thirty seconds to three minutes, and then repeat on the other foot.

5. If it's hard to reach your own foot, you can ask a friend to massage this point for you.

16
JUNE

PROPER PLACE

View some Chinese landscape paintings. Notice how much of the canvas is devoted to empty space and sky and the relative smallness of human beings within the immensity of the natural world. This reflects the wisdom of the Tao.

17
JUNE

SEXUAL ENERGY

Like good food and ample exercise, physical intimacy and touch provide nourishment for your human body-mind. It's natural to desire and enjoy healthy sexual relationships. It's also natural to appreciate how sexual energy flows within your body, with or without a partner.

18
JUNE

BODY SCAN

1. Sit comfortably or lie down.

2. Place your attention at the crown of your head. Maintain a gentle focus here for three to five seconds, simply noticing any sensations that arise without the addition of mental commentary.

3. Shift your attention from the crown to your face, once again noticing, with an attitude of benevolent indifference, any sensations that arise.

4. Continue in this way to scan all the parts of your body—neck, shoulders, arms, torso, hips, legs, and feet.

5. When you've reached your toes, reverse the order, moving slowly back up to the crown of your head.

6. Move at a rate that allows you to complete one full scan—top to bottom to top—in around eight minutes.

19
JUNE

GOLD NUGGETS

Imagine your sitting-bones to be nuggets of gold: heavy and bright. When you're sitting in a chair or on the floor, feel the natural pull of gravity as a return of these precious gems to their home in the earth.

20
JUNE

*One who is filled with the Tao
is like a newborn child.*

TAO TE CHING, **CHAPTER 55**

21
JUNE

CREATING A TAOIST ALTAR

If you'd like to create a traditional Taoist altar, here's what to include:

- A picture or statue of a Taoist Immortal or deity that inspires you.

- A lamp of some kind, which represents the Light of Tao.

- Two candles, placed to the left and right of the lamp, which represent the sun and moon.

- Three small cups: one filled with water, one with tea, and one with uncooked rice. These symbolize yin, yang, and the union of yin and yang.

- Five plates of fruit and bowls of food, which represent the five elements.

- An incense burner along with three sticks of incense, which symbolize the lower *tan-t'ien* and the three treasures of inner alchemy.

22
JUNE
SHRINE

Ultimately, the entire cosmos, including your precious human body-mind, is your altar. Each time you encounter something beautiful or feel inspired, express your devotion with a gentle smile or by bringing the palms of your hands together at your heart-center.

23
JUNE
TRANSFORMATIONS

When warmed by the sun, ice melts into water and then evaporates into steam.
   When warmed by the sun of mindful attention, frozen blocks of anger, grief, fear, or jealousy can melt, flow, and evaporate.

24
JUNE
—
CONSULTING THE *I-CHING*

Consulting the *I-Ching* is a way to receive guidance about present or future life activities or decisions.

The hexagrams represent all the objects/events in the cosmos and their evolving circumstances. A particular hexagram can offer clues on how best to align with earthly and heavenly influences to support an auspicious outcome.

To consult the *I-Ching* using the coin method:

1. Hold in mind a question or dilemma that you have.

2. Toss three coins and, using the *I-Ching* chart, record the resulting trigram.

3. Toss the three coins five more times, building the trigram from the bottom to the top, like a building on its foundation.

4. Read the commentary on the resulting trigram in light of your question.

25
JUNE

CLEARING THE CACHE

Entering the space of not-knowing, through Taoist meditation or aimless wandering, is like clearing the cache of your computer. It frees up space and increases efficiency effortlessly.

When the past is released, Presence naturally shines.

26
JUNE

Getting or losing: how to tell which is which?
I lean here smiling softly to the breeze.
The spider so pleased with his artful web
has netted only fallen blossoms,
not a single bug to eat.

—YUAN MEI (TRANSLATED BY J. P. SEATON)

27
JUNE

LETTERS ON WATER

Perceptions, thoughts, sensations, coming and going, moment by moment, are as ephemeral as letters written on the surface of water.

Is what happened yesterday or even two minutes ago any more tangible than the events in your dream last night?

28
JUNE

PLACING DEITIES IN THE BODY

Imagine placing a miniature version of a deity or object from the natural world within your body.

Some possibilities include a tree, a mountain, a river, a waterfall, sunshine, mist, a rainbow, a crystal or gemstone, a star, a planet, or a galaxy.

You could also choose a favorite animal (horse, lion, dolphin, hummingbird) or an inspiring Taoist immortal or deity.

Imagine a delicate, ephemeral, light-filled version of your chosen object in a specific place in your body (e.g., in your heart-center, your lower *tan-t'ien*, or the soles of your feet).

Notice and enjoy the feeling that this imaginary being creates.

After a couple minutes, allow the image to dissolve while retaining the feeling.

29
JUNE

RELATIVITY OF TIME

A mayfly's average life span is twenty-four hours. Large turtles can live four hundred to five hundred years. This means that a single turtle can witness 182,500 mayfly generations!

So what's the truth of a human life span: Is it long or short?

30
JUNE

HAVE A GIGGLE-FEST

For an hour or two (or an entire evening) place yourself in the presence of things that you know will make you grin, chuckle, giggle, or belly laugh until you cry, all of which are great for releasing physical tensions and lifting your spirit. If you need inspiration, cue up:

- *Far Side* cartoons
- *Seinfeld* or *South Park*
- *I Heart Huckabees*
- A Monty Python film
- *The Truman Show*
- *Sister Act*
- *Dolemite Is My Name*
- Funny animal videos
- Your favorite comedian

Whatever it is that you know will tickle your funny bone, do that! Be amazed and amused by how silly humans can be and inspired by the infinite creativity of the Tao.

JULY

1
JULY

We should never forget:
What we are looking for is what is looking.

—WEI WU WEI, *POSTHUMOUS PIECES*

2
JULY

RAINBOW

Sunlight flowing through a crystal becomes a rainbow of colors—white light refracting into red, orange, yellow, green, blue, indigo, and violet.

Just so, the Light of Tao appears as the ten thousand things (all the objects/events of the cosmos).

3
JULY
FASTING OF THE HEART-MIND

Chuang Tzu (translated by Thomas Merton) has said:

"The goal of fasting is inner unity. This means hearing, but not with the ear; hearing, but not with the understanding; hearing with the spirit, with your whole being."

To explore these three ways of hearing:

1. Notice a sound that's registered by your ears.

2. Notice the activity of your mind in relation to this sound: how it applies a name ("Oh, that's a bird singing") and perhaps also some commentary ("That's beautiful but not quite as nice as the birdsong I heard yesterday").

3. See if you can release the naming and mental commentary, forgoing intellectual interpretation, and instead listen with your *whole being*.

4
JULY

WHAT IS IT?

No matter how completely you describe yourself, there will always be something essential that evades description, which is inconceivable and inexpressible.

What is this "something essential"? Don't try to answer with your mind. Instead, find it in your inner experience, right now.

5
JULY

MEETING OF HEAVEN AND EARTH #2

1. Stand with your feet shoulder-width apart and arms hanging naturally by your sides.

2. Press down gently through the soles of your feet, as though you were growing roots.

3. With an inhalation, swing your arms and hands out to the side and then overhead, like a tree drawing sap up into its branches.

4. As you exhale, float your palms downward toward the crown of your head and then a couple inches in front of your torso, as though drawing sky/heaven-energy through the core of your body along the front of your spine.

5. Repeat this cycle ten times, or more if you'd like.

6
JULY

MURMURATION

Almost miraculously, a large flock of starlings, tens of thousands of birds, can move as one. Schools of fish have this same capacity to move as though they are a single organism.

Just so, the cells of your human body move as one.

7
JULY

Because [Tao] is Great means it is everywhere.
Being everywhere means it is eternal.
Being eternal means everything returns to it.

TAO TE CHING, **CHAPTER 25**

8
JULY

GRATITUDE

Cultivate your capacity for wonder, awe, and gratitude—for a beautiful sunset, a tiny ladybug, or the most spectacular of scientific achievements (airplanes, running water, brain surgery).

When feeling appreciative or inspired by something, bring the palms of your hands together, tune into the energy of your heart-center, and allow your entire being to smile.

If you'd like, you can say (out loud or internally): "Yes, thank you!" or "I bow to you in gratitude."

Notice how nourishing it is to bathe in the energy of gratitude.

9
JULY
—
YIN AND YANG

Whatever your birth or adopted gender, your body contains both *yin-ch'i* and *yang-ch'i*, both feminine and masculine energy. When these are in harmony, there are health and vitality.

And, in your essence, you are neither male nor female but rather the eternal Tao.

AT THE MOVIES

To understand the relationship between Tao and the ten thousand things, consider the relationship between a movie screen and the images projected on the screen:

- Could the images appear without the screen? No, the screen is necessary for the movie to appear.

- Is the screen in any way affected by the images? No, the screen itself is not altered in any way by the content of the movie. The screen exists before the movie begins, while the movie is playing, and after the movie is finished.

As you move through your day, consider the possibility that the unchanging Tao is like a movie screen and worldly activities/events are akin to movie images. Notice how this transforms your experience.

11
JULY

EQUANIMITY

For a full day, experiment with not being bothered by anything and, if you do feel bothered, not being bothered by that.

Don't take things personally. Instead, cultivate an attitude of benevolent indifference, letting worldly events flow like water droplets off the feathers of a swan.

12
JULY

TRAVELOGUE

What's it like to have a dog's sense of smell, or a bat's fancy echolocation—navigating via reflected sound?

Chuang Tzu might suggest that having a different perceptual system is akin to traveling to a foreign country; suddenly, you're in a completely different world!

13
JULY
CH'I BALL

1. Stand or sit comfortably, with your spine upright.

2. Rub the palms of your hands together for fifteen to twenty seconds.

3. Hold your hands with the palms facing one another and around ten inches apart at the level of your lower *tan-t'ien*.

4. Imagine that your hands are holding a beautiful sphere of light, whatever color feels most healing and/or enjoyable. Turn this sphere of life-force energy over in your hands, move it side to side, or let it compress and then expand.

5. Imagine this sphere of light to be the most precious thing in the universe. Fall in love with it.

6. After a few minutes, imagine the *ch'i*-ball merging with the space of your lower *tan-t'ien*.

14
JULY

[The Master] is there to help all of creation,
and doesn't abandon even the smallest creature.
This is called embracing the light.

TAO TE CHING, **CHAPTER 27**

15
JULY

LOVE LETTER FROM THE PAST

The starlight appearing in the night sky has traveled many light-years to reach your eyes. It's what the stars looked like a very long time ago.

Even though they may no longer exist, you can still appreciate the beauty of their display.

16
JULY

FORGIVENESS #1

1. Sit comfortably or lie down. Gently close your eyes.

2. Think of someone whom you feel ready to forgive or someone to whom you'd like to apologize and from whom you'd like to request forgiveness.

3. Imagine a miniature version of this person (no more than an inch tall) in the form of light, like a little fairy.

4. Imagine this fairylike version of them floating in your lower *tan-t'ien* or heart-center, whichever you'd prefer.

5. In whatever way makes sense to you, ask for or offer forgiveness, and imagine the tiny being gratefully receiving or willingly offering it.

6. To end the exercise, allow the light-being to dissolve and merge with the light of your heart-center or lower *tan-t'ien*.

17
JULY
SWADDLING

Wear clothing made of natural fibers: cotton, wool, hemp, cashmere, alpaca, flax-linen, silk, or jute. These make it easier for your skin to breathe. Notice how you feel internally when you are more comfortable externally. How does it affect your mood?

18
JULY
EMOTION AND SENSATION

1. Sit quietly, and gently close your eyes.

2. Become interested in physical sensations—how your body feels from the inside.

3. Each time you notice a particular sensation, say "touch" to yourself, as a way of identifying it as a physical sensation.

4. Be interested as well in emotional energy—feelings of anger, fear, sadness, shame, frustration, and so on.

5. Each time you notice an emotion, say "feel" to yourself as a way of identifying it as an emotion.

6. Continue for two to three minutes, clarifying the difference between physical sensations and emotional energy and noticing when they intermingle.

19
JULY
—

FRIENDLY UNIVERSE

Your human body-mind is not an isolated fragment, disconnected from its surroundings and needing to struggle for survival in a hostile universe.

Instead, it is interconnected with all-that-is. When you understand this deeply, the universe becomes your friend.

20
JULY
—

SIGNAL AND RECEIVER

Radio waves exist independently of the radios that receive and transmit them. Electricity exists independently of the light bulbs it illuminates.

Consider the possibility that, in the same way, Awareness—the Light of Tao—exists independently of human body-minds.

21
JULY

The soft and pliable overcomes the hard and inflexible.

TAO TE CHING, **CHAPTER 36**

22
JULY

ROCKING THE *TAN-T'IEN*

1. Lie down on the floor, faceup.

2. Hinge your knees so the soles of your feet rest flat on the floor, hip-distance apart.

3. Support your head with a pillow, if you'd like, or rest it directly on the floor.

4. Rest the palms of your hands on your lower abdomen.

5. With an exhalation, draw your navel down toward the floor, tucking your pelvis and curling your tailbone slightly up toward the ceiling.

6. With the next inhalation, allow your pelvis to return to neutral.

7. Repeat this movement eight to ten times; then interlace your fingers behind your head, elbows dropping toward the floor, and repeat another eight to ten times.

23
JULY

—

NATURALLY SWEET

Taoism encourages us to take good care of the physical body.

One step in this direction is to gradually replace refined sugar with natural sweeteners such as raw honey, pure maple syrup, coconut sugar, date syrup, stevia, and blackstrap molasses. As you make these changes, note improvements in your body as well as your mind.

24
JULY

ROPE AND SNAKE

Imagine entering a shed at dusk. In the declining light, you see a large snake curled up in the corner and, in fear, run out of the shed.

The next morning, with the sun shining brightly, you return to the shed and discover that what you thought was a snake was just a coiled rope.

Now use this metaphor to understand the relationship between your human body-mind and the idea of a separate self:

- The coiled rope represents your ever-changing body-mind.

- The snake illusion is the idea of a separate self, an unchanging limited "me" superimposed onto the body-mind.

To break the illusion, notice that the ever-changing body-mind is perceived by *you*—unchanging Awareness.

25
JULY

MISTY MOUNTAINS

In how they conceal and then reveal, misty mountains are evocative and flirtatious.

Just so, the Light of Tao may seem to be playing hide-and-seek. But you know it's just a game, and soon the sunlight will reveal the mountain in all her glory.

26
JULY

INNER SMILE #3

1. Find a quiet place to sit or lie down.

2. Take a few deep, slow breaths, and relax your jaw completely, as though you were saying "ahh."

3. Rest your attention lightly at the center of your forehead. Let your attention drift back to the very center of your skull, resting your focus gently there.

4. Smile gently with your entire being as well as your mouth. Allow your eyes to become smiling eyes.

5. With these smiling eyes, turn your gaze inward, directing smile-energy to someplace in your body that has an injury, an illness, or numbness or just a place you haven't said hello to in a while.

6. End by sending smile-energy to your lower *tan-t'ien*.

27
JULY

HUMILITY

True humility emerges naturally with the dissolution of the arrogance/humiliation polarity: no longer better than others and no longer worse than others. Instead, you realize yourself to be both tiny (as a body-mind) and immense (as the Light of Tao), simultaneously.

28
JULY

The highest good is not to seek to do good,
but to allow yourself to become it.

TAO TE CHING, **CHAPTER 38**

29
JULY

MODERATION

Satisfy your physical and psychological needs and honor the natural impulse for celebration and exploration without going overboard. Don't expect worldly objects/events to deliver the happiness that you most deeply desire. They weren't designed for that!

30
JULY

RANDOM ACTS OF KINDNESS

In a playful spirit, practice random acts of kindness.

Bring wonder and awe, beauty, hope, tenderness, a shared smile, or a helping hand to friends, relatives, or (the most fun!) complete strangers.

Offer your seat to someone on the bus. Donate flowers to a nursing home. Give an unexpected compliment. Plant a tree. Smile at someone who looks sad.

Offer this generosity in the spirit of a true gift, with no expectation of getting something in return.

Let these random acts of kindness emerge from the understanding that there are no real "others," that we enjoy a shared essence, and in a real sense are "all in this together."

31
JULY

PRESENCE

Inner stillness (the absence of agitation) is also known as Presence. It's letting go of the extraneous to settle into what's most essential.

Presence is akin to enjoying an exquisitely high signal-to-noise ratio. And it's the greatest gift we can give to those around us and to the world.

AUGUST

1
AUGUST

ONENESS

An accomplished composer who attends a concert might notice the sound of individual instruments, but mostly they will abandon themselves fully to the flow of the music, experiencing it as a whole.

What is it that allows for *many* to be experienced as *one*?

2
AUGUST

EXCHANGING ENERGY WITH A TREE

1. Stand ten to fifteen feet away from a tree (or plant) that makes your heart sing.

2. Inhale fully, and then, with the exhale, press the palms of your hands downward from your lower ribs in the direction of your big toes.

3. At the same time, imagine releasing toxic/stagnant energy through your big toes into the tree's roots.

4. With the next inhale, swing your arms out to the side and overhead, palms facing skyward, in a gesture of gathering the blessing emanating from the tree's branches.

5. As you exhale, use your palms to draw this blessing into the crown of your head and all the way down the central channel.

6. Repeat eight to ten times, or more if you'd like.

3
AUGUST

———

[The Tao] gives them life without wanting to posses them,
and cares for them expecting nothing in return.
It is their master, but it does not seek to dominate them.
This is called the dark and mysterious virtue.

TAO TE CHING, **CHAPTER 51**

4
AUGUST

CREATIVE POTENCY

Creative/sexual energy (*ch'ing*)—one of Taoism's Three Treasures—is what initiates and powers the creation of symphonies, poems, gourmet meals, and new scientific discoveries as well as physical offspring.

What are your favorite ways of expressing your creative potency?

5
AUGUST

SEATED STANDING MEDITATION

You can practice standing meditation while sitting on a bus or train or at home reading or watching television in a comfy recliner. Here's how:

1. If there are armrests, then rest your elbows on them to keep your arms slightly away from your torso. If not, rest your hands on your thighs.

2. Rotate your hands so the palms are facing your lower *tan-t'ien*, and imagine that you're gently hugging a balloon.

3. If you're reading, hold the book or tablet in front of your chest with your elbows lifted slightly and palms facing your middle *tan-t'ien*. Once again, imagine that you're hugging a balloon between your inner arms and torso.

6
AUGUST

A poet who allows words to emerge from the depths of their Being will speak, via their poems, directly to the Being of the reader.

Across continents and millennia, such poems will survive. Why? Because they are rooted in eternity.

7
AUGUST

AVOCADO-RASPBERRY SMOOTHIE

Healthy fats are vital for the human brain and nervous system, which, in turn, offer support for your *ch'i-kung* and Taoist meditation practice.

Consider preparing this nutritious and delicious treat, featuring healthy fats (avocado) along with nutrient-rich berries, hydrating coconut water, and the smooth energy of matcha.

½ avocado
½ banana
½ cup fresh or frozen raspberries

½ to 1 cup young coconut water
¼ cup cream, half-and-half, or almond milk
1 tablespoon pure maple syrup
½ teaspoon matcha powder
Pinch of cinnamon

Mix all the ingredients in a food processor or blender, adjusting liquid amounts as desired, for a spoon-able pudding or a drinkable smoothie.

Enjoy!

8
AUGUST
RESURRECTION

A fun thing to do, as you move through your day, is to imagine everyone you see as being a five-year-old child, exhibiting innocence, freshness, curiosity, and playfulness.

What were *you* like as a five-year-old?

9
AUGUST

—

The Tao never acts with force,
yet there is nothing that it cannot do.

TAO TE CHING, **CHAPTER 37**

10
AUGUST

—

STAYING HOME

When you notice strong feelings of attraction or repulsion toward another human being, it's possible to allow the energy of these emotions to flow freely, like river rapids through a forest, while remaining centered in yourself.

For instance, if the driver in the next lane has just swerved into your lane and you feel a surge of anger, take a few deep, slow breaths, and welcome the energy of this emotion without collapsing into it.

Or if someone you have a crush on is walking toward you and you feel a surge of sexual arousal, smile gently and fully experience and enjoy this sensation without needing to direct it outward.

11
AUGUST
—
WHOSE CLOCK?

If you're living in the United States, it's always tomorrow in Australia.

If you're living in Australia, it's always yesterday in the United States.

Does this mean that time travel is actually possible? Or, as Chuang Tzu might point out, that even time is relative.

12
AUGUST
—
TRUE LOVE

In true love, the presumed boundary between self and other dissolves. You see yourself in the eyes of the beloved and experience the truth of your oneness—your non-separation. You recognize intimately your shared origin.

How wonderful!

13

AUGUST

OPPOSITES IN UNION

1. Lie down with your knees hinged and feet flat on the floor.

2. If you'd like, place a small pillow under your head.

3. Interlace your fingers over your right shin or the back of your right thigh to draw that knee gently toward your chest.

4. Release the right foot back to the floor and repeat on the left side.

5. Draw both knees toward your chest, and rock gently side to side (as though rocking an infant in their cradle) with your knees and head moving in opposite directions. As your knees drift slightly to the left, allow your head to move to the right, and vice versa.

This movement helps synchronize the two hemispheres of your brain, allowing logic and intuition to be integrated.

14
AUGUST

HIDDEN AND REVEALED

Imagine there's a treasure chest filled with gold coins buried in your backyard, but you don't know that it's there. Are you rich or not?

Just so, you *are* the Light of Tao, though until you realize this directly, it's not quite real.

15
AUGUST

*Rivers and seas are rulers
of the streams of hundreds of valleys
because of the power of their low position.*

TAO TE CHING, **CHAPTER 66**

16
AUGUST

LIMINAL SPACES

1. Pay attention to the boundary between night and day or between waking and sleeping.

2. At dawn or dusk, can you identify the exact moment when night transforms into day or day into night?

3. Can you notice when the first star becomes visible? Or when the wafer-thin moon dissolves fully into sunlight?

4. Ask yourself:

   ◈ What remains constant, as night and day cycle back and forth?

   ◈ What remains constant—as waking, as dreaming, and in a deep-sleep cycle—through each twenty-four-hour period?

   ◈ Contemplate these questions as you sit quietly, or use them as a topic for a journal entry.

   ◈ Let the answers reveal themselves naturally, as they're ready.

17
AUGUST
—
TRUE DESTINATION

The North Star is a beacon to help sailors plot their course, but it's not their destination.

In the same way, understand the value of scriptures, including the *Tao Te Ching*. They can only guide you to the true destination, which is already within you.

18
AUGUST
—
SUNNY AND SHADY

Like the shady and sunny side of a mountain or the shady and sunny side of a city street, opposites always arise together, even if one is temporarily hidden from view.

Can you see how this is true?

19
AUGUST

FEEDING THE DEITIES

Just for fun, as you sit down to a meal:

1. Imagine that each of the 100 trillion cells within your human body is the abode of a deity: a saint or sage, god or goddess, archangel or Taoist immortal. Imagine these deities dancing ecstatically or walking peacefully within their tiny homes.

2. With each bite of food, imagine that you're feeding these deities. As you swallow, you're sending tiny care packages of their favorite foods—what's most delicious and nourishing, what brings them greatest delight. Imagine them gratefully receiving these gifts of great nourishment.

3. Take delight in this fanciful practice, and understand that these imagined deities symbolize wise and empowered aspects of yourself.

20
AUGUST

WISDOM OF SUCCULENTS

Notice the wisdom of succulents, how storing water efficiently in their leaves allows them to survive a drought.

In your own life, too, understand when the time is right for gathering and storing resources.

21
AUGUST

Act by not acting;
do by not doing.
Enjoy the plain and simple.
Find that greatness in the small.

TAO TE CHING, **CHAPTER 63**

22
AUGUST

ENTHUSIASM

Follow the thread of your enthusiasm (what piques your curiosity or brings you joy) without being overly attached to the objects, events, or people you may encounter along the way.

This is how to flow with the Tao.

23
AUGUST

CANDLE FLAME

If your mind tends toward being scattered or easily distracted, this is a useful way of cultivating the ability to concentrate.

1. Sit with a candle flame at eye level, about two feet away.

2. Rest your gaze gently on the flame.

3. After a couple minutes, close your eyes and perceive the flame's after-image, staying relaxed to maintain it for as long as you can.

4. Rather than focusing on the flame or its afterimage, *imagine* the flame, in as much detail as you can, in your mind's eye.

5. Open your eyes again and continue gazing at the flame itself.

6. Contemplate the relationship between these three: the flame, its after-image, and the imagined image.

24
AUGUST

—

PUTTING DOWN THE BACKPACK

Sit down to meditate as though putting down a heavy backpack after a long hike: It feels so good just to relax!

It's a release, a letting-go, not something gained or achieved.

25
AUGUST

WAKEFUL RELAXATION

1. Find a comfortable place (floor, couch, or bed) to lie down on your back.

2. Close your eyes, and release the weight of your body fully into what is supporting it.

3. Direct your attention to your left foot, flooding it with energy/awareness; then surrender those sensations completely.

4. Continue in this way for every part of your body, from feet to head.

5. Flood your whole body in a single field of energy/awareness, feeling the entirety of your physical form bathed in this unified field of radiance.

6. Enjoy feeling deeply relaxed while remaining awake.

26
AUGUST

FLYING

Imagine soaring, circling, spiraling through the sky like a hawk or eagle, buoyed by the wind's invisible currents.

This is the position of the Taoist sage, whose freedom emerges from a view that remains deep, wide, and vast.

27
AUGUST

Whether to oppose or conform is up to the mind; on the peaks of a thousand mountains, one sings and hums forever.

—**LIU I-MING** (TRANSLATED BY THOMAS CLEARY IN *AWAKENING TO THE TAO*)

28
AUGUST
—
EVERYWHERE

When you see yourself in all things, you realize, "I am everywhere."

If you are everywhere, how can there possibly be any sense of lack? What could possibly be missing?

29
AUGUST
—
HARMONY

Each of your body's organs (heart, liver, kidneys, etc.) plays a vital role in its overall health and vitality.

Just so, each organism (plant, mineral, or animal) contributes a unique song to nature's symphony.

What is *your* unique song?

30
AUGUST

OBJECTS PERCEIVED AND IMAGINED

1. Choose a small object to gaze upon: a houseplant, a crystal, a coffee mug.

2. Continue looking at the object for thirty seconds or so.

3. Close your eyes and *imagine* the object in as much detail as you can.

4. Allow the internal image of the object to dissolve.

5. Ask yourself, Where does the image go after it has dissolved?

6. Don't look for the answer in your mind, but rather *experience* it.

7. Ask yourself, As the image dissolves, do I dissolve? Who or what is this "I" that remains, as perceived or imagined objects come and go?

31
AUGUST
WAVING

Waves are the movement of ocean water.

Flames are the movement of fire.

The ten thousand things (including *your* human body-mind) are the movement of the Tao.

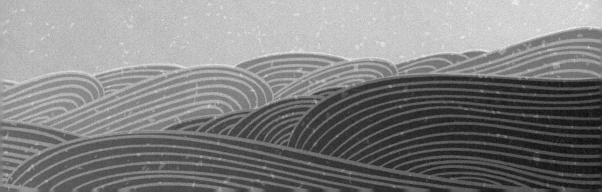

SEPTEMBER

1
SEPTEMBER

BUTTERFLY DREAM

Chuang Tzu dreamt that he was a butterfly. Upon waking, he wondered, "Am I a man who has just dreamt I was a butterfly, or a butterfly now dreaming that I am a man?"

Be curious about the various identities that you assume within your waking and dreaming worlds.

2
SEPTEMBER

The rigid and stiff will be broken.
The soft and yielding will overcome.

TAO TE CHING, **CHAPTER 76**

3
SEPTEMBER
—
FREE RANGE

1. Stand or sit comfortably.

2. Curl the fingers of your right hand into a tight fist. Hold for five seconds and then release, allowing your fingers to uncurl, then fully extend, and then relax.

3. Repeat for your left hand, curling your fingers into a tight bud and then opening them like the petals of a blossoming flower.

4. Curl both fists tightly, hold, and then fully unfurl the fingers.

5. Tense every muscle in your body, from head to toe, at the same time, and then fully release.

6. Enjoy energized relaxation—not too tight, not too loose. Can you resurrect the capacity to move freely between contraction and release?

4
SEPTEMBER

GOLDEN OPPORTUNITY

When you've been scattered or lost in distraction and suddenly *become aware* of this, it is a golden opportunity.

In such a moment, you've already withdrawn the arrow of attention from its external focus. Now simply rest in and as the undisturbed unity of Awareness.

5
SEPTEMBER

HORSE AND RIDER

A primary axiom of *ch'i-gong* practice is that energy follows attention. Where you place your attention, life-force energy (*ch'i*) gathers.

Like a rider on a horse, attention provides direction for the movement of life-force energy.

6
SEPTEMBER

SHARING THE WEALTH

1. Sit comfortably or lie down.

2. Become aware of some place in your body that feels comfortable, balanced, refreshed, at ease. Appreciate these pleasant sensations.

3. Let the energy of the pleasant sensation emanate into surrounding tissues and organs, sharing the wealth of its comfort and ease.

4. Allow the pleasant sensation to flow into places that are injured, diseased, or numb. Feel or imagine this healing balm gently enveloping and soaking into those places.

5. Continue for five to ten minutes, or longer if you'd like.

6. In similar fashion, you can emanate peace and joy into your surrounding worldly environment, bathing all those who share it with stealth blessings.

7
SEPTEMBER
———

SYMPATHETIC JOY

Instead of feeling jealous of another person's good fortune, cultivate sympathetic joy—a resonant celebration rooted in nondual wisdom.

Each time you welcome and appreciate health and prosperity, wherever it appears, the self/other duality begins to soften.

8
SEPTEMBER
———

The nondual reality that we've been searching for, is already present as our own awareness. This means it's not a concept to be learned, it's an ever-present actuality that is to be recognized.

—JOHN SEFTON, *IDENTIFYING NONDUALITY*

9
SEPTEMBER

DISSOLVED AND RE-CREATED

Moment by moment, the cells of your human body are dying and being reborn. This is what makes growth and healing possible.

In similar fashion, be willing to let go of rigidly held beliefs and unexamined assumptions, at least for a while.

Enter a space of not-knowing. Trust that you can pick up the beliefs and assumptions if they prove useful.

In similar fashion, wear your worldly identities lightly. Celebrate spontaneity, fluidity, playfulness. Be willing, in every moment, to dissolve and re-create yourself.

Appreciate the kaleidoscopic transformations happening continuously in bodies, minds, and worlds.

And realize your Self as the unchanging witness of all such transformations.

10
SEPTEMBER

—

NOURISHMENT

Each time you drink a glass of water, you're drinking the lakes and rivers of the world. With each slice of orange or bite of broccoli, mineral-rich soil, sunshine, and rain are providing nourishment.

11
SEPTEMBER

—

CENTRAL CHANNEL

Imagine your spinal cord as a thread of golden silk.
Imagine a river of liquid light flowing up the center of this golden thread.
And within the river of liquid light is luminous emptiness.

12

SEPTEMBER

ALTERNATE-NOSTRIL BREATHING

1. Sit comfortably and tune into the natural flow of your breathing.

2. Feel the life-force energy (the *ch'i*) that is within the breath, like an electric current flowing through a wire.

3. Use the thumb of your right hand to gently close your right nostril, and inhale softly through your left nostril.

4. Use the ring finger of your right hand to gently close your left nostril, and exhale softly through your right nostril.

5. Inhale through your right nostril.

6. Once again, use your thumb to close your right nostril, and exhale through your left nostril.

7. Complete five full rounds, and then sit quietly for a few minutes.

13
SEPTEMBER

NATURAL MEDITATION

There are many meditation *techniques*, which are tools for cultivating the mind's strength and pliability, like an athlete cultivating physical strength and flexibility.

Natural meditation is who you are essentially and effortlessly: Pure Awareness, the Light of Tao.

14
SEPTEMBER

THREAD OF CONTINUITY

Be curious about the moment of falling asleep. As you relax deeply, allowing the perceptions of the waking world to dissolve, can you notice the emergence of dream imagery?

What is the thread that links the waking and the dreaming worlds?

15
SEPTEMBER

—

Stop talking,
meditate in silence,
blunt your sharpness,
release your worries,
harmonize your inner light,
and become one with the dust.
Doing this is called the dark and mysterious identity.

TAO TE CHING, **CHAPTER 56**

16
SEPTEMBER

SENSATION UNFOLDING

1. Sit comfortably or lie down; then close your eyes.

2. Tune into physical sensations—your direct felt experience of the body.

3. Notice sensations appearing, transforming, and dissolving, moment by moment.

4. See that there are no clearly defined boundaries to sensations. They have no precise, fixed location, but rather dance and merge with the space around them.

5. Notice any tendency to engage in mental commentary about a sensation or overlay an image or belief about "my body."

6. Stay with the innocence, purity, and nakedness of physical sensation without belief, judgment, or commentary.

7. Let sensations point back to the Awareness within which they arise and dissolve, and know this as your true identity.

17
SEPTEMBER
—
BELOVED

Can you gaze upon a tree, a rock, a waterfall, or a ladybug as though gazing upon your beloved with that same loving tenderness?

Can you see all beings as your beloved?

18
SEPTEMBER
—
SUCTION

1. Just for fun, suck your thumb, as an infant does. Or suck your cheeks, imitating the pulsing mouth of a fish. Continue for twenty to thirty seconds. Become familiar with these suction sensations so you can use them as a template for activating your feet.

2. With an inhalation, swing your arms out to the sides and overhead. At the same time, see if you can imagine a similar suction in the soles of your feet.

3. Picture yourself drawing earth energy through the soles of your feet to the lower *tan-t'ien*, like a tree drawing sap up through its roots. Or imagine you're drinking a thick milkshake through a long straw, drawing nectar from the center of the earth and then tasting its sweetness on the roof of your mouth.

19

SEPTEMBER

COSMIC WOMB

When your whole being is suffused with peace, calm, quietude—and *ch'i* is abundant—then a subtle form of "breathing" directly from the lower *tan-t'ien* may naturally emerge. Life-force energy is drawn as though via an umbilical cord directly from your cosmic mother.

20

SEPTEMBER

INSIDE AND ALL AROUND

Be amazed by the vast intelligence operating within your human body.
Be amazed by the vast intelligence of the whole cosmos.
Understand both as the Light of Tao expressing her infinite creativity.

21
SEPTEMBER
—

Sometimes there is no sun or moon in the sky, but there is never an absence of the essence of seeing that sees the sun and moon.

—LIU TUNG-PIN (TRANSLATED BY THOMAS CLEARY IN *THE SECRET OF THE GOLDEN FLOWER*)

22
SEPTEMBER
—

THE MARVELOUS MUNG BEAN

Mung beans are a great thing to add to your diet. They're nutritious and easily digested, inexpensive, and delicious in both sweet and savory dishes.

To cook: Soak the dried beans for an hour. Add new water and bring to a boil; then simmer for forty-five to sixty minutes on the stovetop until tender.

For a nice curry, add steamed sweet potato, cauliflower, and green peas to the cooked mung beans; flavor with coconut oil, cumin, coriander, cardamom, and turmeric; and serve on a bed of brown rice or quinoa.

For a sweet treat, bathe the cooked mung beans in coconut milk; spice with cinnamon, cardamom, and anise seeds; sweeten with pure maple syrup; and top with raisins, shredded coconut, and/or pecans.

23
SEPTEMBER

STAINED-GLASS WINDOWS

Imagine your eyes to be the stained-glass windows of a temple.
And your other sense organs, too.
The Light of Tao flowing through them creates the world you perceive.

24
SEPTEMBER

FLOATING BONES

Instead of assuming that it is your bones that provide the support for your muscles and connective tissue, play with flipping this model on its head, allowing your bones to float.

Feel into the space within the joints of your body: finger joints, toe joints, wrists, ankles, elbows, knees, shoulders, hips, and the vertebrae of your spine.

As you access a sense of spaciousness within the joints, imagine the bones floating away from the joint. Feel each vertebra floating independently of all the others.

Now notice how you feel, physically and emotionally.

In this experiment, you allow the rigid to be supported by the soft and fluid—the less substantial—rather than the other way around.

25
SEPTEMBER
—
GARDEN

If you're able and so inclined, plant some fruit trees, cultivate a vegetable garden, or grow herbs in a window box. Care for these plants well, and then, at harvest time, enjoy the fruits (and/or veggies) of your labor. *Yum!*

26
SEPTEMBER
—
ETERNITY

Perennials are plants that come back every year; they last a long time. Eternity is not long-lasting but rather *timeless*.

The Tao is eternal. It belongs to a wholly different "dimension," which is the source of space and time.

27
SEPTEMBER

TRANSFORMING YOUR INNER CRITIC

1. Welcome the voice of the inner critic, and any emotions that it triggers, with an attitude of benevolent indifference.

2. Experiment with hearing the inner critic's words as just sound, like the sound of birdsong, or a symphony, just not quite as harmonious.

3. Understand the inner critic to be just one member of a committee. And now give the floor to your inner advocate, the one who offers words of encouragement and support.

4. Even better, allow words of kindness and compassion to emerge from the wisdom at the core of your Being:

"I love you unconditionally."

"You are primordially pure."

"I love and accept you exactly as you are."

28
SEPTEMBER

—

One who seeks knowledge learns something new every day.
One who seeks the Tao unlearns something new every day.
Less and less remains until you arrive at non-action.
When you arrive at non-action,
nothing will be left undone.

TAO TE CHING, **CHAPTER 48**

29
SEPTEMBER

—

FRAGRANCE

Scents have a powerful effect on the limbic system, the part of the brain associated with memory and emotion.

Be curious about which scents affect you most deeply. Which are energizing or soothing? Which connect you with a childhood memory?

30

SEPTEMBER

FINDING CENTER

1. Stand with your feet shoulder-width apart, toes pointing forward, and arms relaxed by your sides.

2. Shift your weight slowly back and forth from your left to your right foot, feeling what it's like to be off-balance in one way or another. Then find center—where you're supporting your weight evenly on your two feet.

3. Do the same thing rocking between your heels and the base of your toes, forward and back. Then find center.

4. Do the same thing rolling inward onto your arches and then outward onto the outer edges of your feet. Then find center.

5. Find center in all three planes of your feet simultaneously.

OCTOBER

1

OCTOBER

TAPPING THE *TAN-T'IEN*

1. Stand with your feet shoulder-width apart.

2. Use the palms of your hands to tap your lower *tan-t'ien* (a couple inches below your navel). Continue tapping, either gently or vigorously, for twenty to thirty seconds.

3. Simply rest your palms gently on the lower *tan-t'ien*, and feel or imagine a warm sun shining within this space.

4. Keep your left hand on your lower *tan-t'ien*, and place your right hand on your middle *tan-t'ien* (the center-chest).

5. Feel the connection between these two energetic spaces: your heart-center and your deep belly. Allow the wisdom of the heart and belly to be in communication.

2
OCTOBER

FIRE AND WATER

In *ch'i-kung* and Chinese medicine, the kidneys are associated with the moon and the water element and the heart with the sun and the fire element. When water and fire unite, they produce great power.

3
OCTOBER

Look for it, and it can't be seen.
Listen for it, and it can't be heard.
Grasp for it, and it can't be caught.

TAO TE CHING, **CHAPTER 14**

4
OCTOBER

FISHNET

Chuang Tzu says that the purpose of a fishnet is to capture a fish. Once the fish is caught, the net can be put aside.

And the same is true for language: Its purpose is to express an idea and then be laid aside.

5
OCTOBER

GOLDEN LIGHT FLOWING #1

1. Stand or sit comfortably.

2. Rub the palms of your hands together for fifteen to twenty seconds.

3. Float your right palm a couple inches away from your torso at the level of your lower right rib cage, where your liver is located.

4. At the same time, float your left hand six to eight inches away from your lower abdomen, with the center of your palm pointing toward your lower *tan-t'ien* (a couple inches below your navel).

5. With your hands in this position, imagine a stream of golden light flowing from your liver to your lower *tan-t'ien*.

6. Continue for one to two minutes, and then rest both palms gently on your lower *tan-t'ien* for a few breaths.

6
OCTOBER
REAL HUMAN BEING

The Taoist sage Liu I-Ming has said: "Recognize the original formless thing, and forge it into an adamantine, indestructible body." This is how to become a real human being.

Contemplate the meaning of these words.

7
OCTOBER
GENEROSITY

Does the sun ever withhold its light? No, it gives itself fully, moment by moment, expressing itself naturally according to its innate capacities.

Be like the sun—offering your gifts freely.

8
OCTOBER

PARCELING THE INHALE

1. Sit comfortably, with your spine in its naturally upright position.

2. Bring your attention to the flow of breathing—the inhalations and exhalations. Just notice its natural rhythm for a minute or two.

3. Divide the inhalation into two packets, stopping briefly in between—inhale halfway, pause, and then inhale the rest of the way.

4. Follow this two-part inhalation with one long smooth exhalation.

5. Repeat five to ten times, and then return to simply observing your breath in its natural rhythm.

6. Once you're comfortable parceling the inhale from a seated position, combine it with walking meditation—a parceled inhale with one step and then a long smooth exhale with the next step.

9
OCTOBER
—

Those who lead people by following the Tao
don't use weapons to enforce their will.
Using force always leads to unseen troubles.

TAO TE CHING, **CHAPTER 30**

10
OCTOBER
—

ENJOY THE FEAST

Will eating the pages of a written menu ever satisfy your hunger?

Honor the *Tao Te Ching* and other sacred texts as useful guides. But don't forget your true reason for visiting the restaurant, which is to enjoy the feast!

LOCATING THE OBSERVER

The location of a human body-mind doesn't imply anything about the location of the observing Awareness.

Consider, for instance, a building's security cameras—one in each room—and the guard who can view all the rooms remotely via screens at the guard station.

Now consider the possibility that:

- Awareness is akin to the security guard.

- And human body-minds are like security cameras: sensory/cognitive recording devices.

Ask yourself:

- Is more than one guard necessary to monitor all the cameras?

- Does damage to one of the security cameras damage the guard?

- If Awareness has no space-time location (because it isn't a "thing"), can it possibly be damaged?

12

OCTOBER

THE SUPREME ART OF WAR

In *The Art of War*, the Chinese sage Sun Tzu suggests that "the supreme art of war is to subdue the enemy without fighting."

How might you apply this wisdom in your life right now?

13

OCTOBER

WIZARDRY

Taoist wizards use rituals and talismans to access subtle realms of power and transform worldly circumstances. But the true source of this and all power is the wholly impersonal Tao.

Does a single wave, however massive, ever own the ocean?

14
OCTOBER

BALANCING THE SITTING BONES

1. Sit on a straight-backed chair that has a firm base, with your feet flat on the floor hip-distance apart. Rest your palms on your thighs.

2. Rock side to side, transferring your weight from one sitting bone to the other. Continue for twenty to thirty seconds.

Alternatively:

1. Sit cross-legged on a thin carpet or hardwood floor. Lift your knees up a bit so you can hook your palms around your upper shins.

2. Rock side to side, letting one sitting bone and then the other lift up off the floor. Continue for twenty to thirty seconds.

3. Notice if one sitting bone feels heavier than the other. If so, be curious about how you might restore balance.

15
OCTOBER
—

Rank and precedence, which the vulgar prize, the Sage stolidly ignores. The revolutions of ten thousand years leave his unity unscathed. The universe itself may pass away, but he will flourish still.

—CHUANG TZU (TRANSLATED BY HERBERT GILES)

16
OCTOBER
—

REMEMBRANCE

Recalling an event that happened yesterday or ten years ago is one thing.

The realization or remembrance of your true nature as the Light of Tao is something else.

The first happens in time. The second *is* the timeless eternal here-now.

17

OCTOBER

RESTFUL MEDITATION

1. Sit comfortably or lie down.

2. Release the weight of your body fully into the support of the chair or ground.

3. Take a few deep, slow breaths, saying "ahh" with the exhalation.

4. Allow thoughts, perceptions, and sensations to come and go, like gentle clouds passing through a vast blue sky. Know that there's no need to get involved with any of them.

5. With serenity, allow your attention to rest in your lower *tan-t'ien* (the deep belly).

6. Feel your belly gently moving with the breath. Feel as though your navel is a third nostril.

7. Enjoy the restful freedom of not needing to do anything.

18
OCTOBER

FROG IN WELL

Can a frog who has lived its entire life in a well truly understand the ocean? Can an insect living and dying during the summer ever truly know what ice is?

Trying to understand the Tao academically and conceptually is the same.

19
OCTOBER

LIGHTHOUSE

A lighthouse helps sailors avoid dangers at sea and reach their destination safely.

Just so, the Taoist sage guides travelers safely to the harbor of lasting peace and happiness.

20
OCTOBER

HAPPY KNEES MEDITATION

1. Sit comfortably in a straight-backed chair with your feet flat on the floor.

2. Rest the tip of your tongue lightly on the roof of your mouth, right behind the upper front teeth. As saliva gathers, swallow it with the intention of sending its energy to your lower *tan-t'ien*.

3. Cup the palms of your hands over your knees, with the middle three fingers curling into the base of the kneecap (right below its lower edge) with light pressure.

4. Rest your attention in the lower *tan-t'ien*, and feel your belly move with the movement of the breath.

5. Notice sensations coming and going, particularly in your knees. Embrace them all with smile-energy.

21
OCTOBER
—

The spirit of emptiness is immortal.
It is called the Great Mother
because it gives birth to Heaven and Earth.
It is like a vapor,
barely seen but always present.
Use it effortlessly.

TAO TE CHING, **CHAPTER 6**

22
OCTOBER
—

WOMB

The Tao is like a womb that births all creatures.

Can you embody this feeling of being the mother of all-that-is, including the mother (the protector and caretaker) of your own precious human body-mind?

23
OCTOBER

DANCING WITH YOUR THYMUS

1. Stand or sit comfortably.

2. Enjoy a few deep, slow breaths, saying "ahh" with the exhalation to relax the muscles of your face, neck, and jaw.

3. Use the three middle fingers of one of your hands to tap lightly at the top of your sternum (breastbone).

4. Behind the sternum lives your thymus, an endocrine gland that supports the immune system by making white blood cells. Say to your thymus: "Hello, my precious thymus. I love you!"

5. Instead of tapping with an even rhythm, tap with a waltz rhythm, and imagine that you're waltzing with your thymus.

6. Continue for thirty to sixty seconds, or longer if you'd like.

24
OCTOBER

INTO-ME-SEE

Play with the word "intimacy" as being the equivalent of "into-me-see."

When you see your own true nature—infinite, eternal, luminous—you will simultaneously know it to be the true nature of all other beings. This is true intimacy.

25
OCTOBER

QUALITY OF LIFE

Spend some time researching where your food comes from. For the produce in your house, can you trace it back to the farm where it was grown?

For meat/eggs, do you know if the animals were raised with sustainable, humane practices?

Whenever possible, try to consider the quality of life of what you consume.

26
OCTOBER

FACIAL MASSAGE

1. Sit comfortably or lie down. Rub the palms of your hands together for fifteen to twenty seconds.

2. Use the ends of your first two fingers to gently massage your right and left temples, moving the fingers (and the loose skin of the temples) in small circles. Continue for thirty to sixty seconds.

3. Use two or three fingers on both hands to massage your forehead, starting in the center, spiraling outward and then back to center.

4. Use loose fists to gently tap the base of your skull, where the skull and neck meet. And now use your thumbs or two fingers to massage the muscles just below the bottom of your skull.

27
OCTOBER

—

The master seeks no possessions.
She learns by unlearning,
thus she is able to understand all things.
This gives her the ability to help all of creation.

TAO TE CHING, **CHAPTER 64**

28
OCTOBER

—

GOLDEN MILK RECIPE

Turmeric (a spice that you may already have in your kitchen) is one of the most well researched of all medicinal herbs and is also a staple of Ayurveda and Chinese herbal medicine. As such, it's a great tool for Taoist body cultivation.

>>>

This recipe is for two servings of turmeric Golden Milk.

2½ cups whole milk or unsweetened almond milk
1½ teaspoons ground turmeric powder
½ teaspoon ground ginger
1 tablespoon coconut oil or ghee
Pinch of black pepper
Pure maple syrup to taste

1. Mix all of the ingredients in a small saucepan and cook over medium heat until it begins to simmer.

2. Pour into mugs and enjoy!

29
OCTOBER

TRUE SOURCE

To seek lasting happiness in any place other than the core of your Being is like trying to quench your thirst with the water of a desert mirage or capture the moon by scooping its reflection from the surface of a lake.

30

OCTOBER

—

DOME OF A TEMPLE

1. Sit comfortably or lie down. Say "ahh" to relax the muscles of your face; and become aware of the inside of your mouth.

2. Imagine the roof of your mouth to be the dome of a temple—high and bright. Feel your whole mouth as open, spacious, and pristine.

3. Imagine your eyes, ears, and nostrils as the beautiful stained-glass windows of this temple.

4. Imagine your teeth as the keys of the temple's organ, piano, or harpsichord.

5. Stay with the image and feeling of your mouth as spacious and bright.

31

OCTOBER

—

COSTUMES

Consider your persona—your worldly identity—to be something like a Halloween costume. Although it can be fun to wear at a party or while trick-or-treating, it feels good to take it off once you return home.

NOVEMBER

1

NOVEMBER

IRRESISTIBLE

As bees are attracted to flowers and tides drawn by the moon's gravitational pull, so it is that we cannot resist the nectar of our own sweetness—the unconditioned peace and joy at the core of our Being.

2

NOVEMBER

CHILD'S POSE

This position, with the forehead softly supported, calms the entire nervous system. Choose the version that's most comfortable for you.

1. Kneel on the floor on all fours.

2. Let your pelvis drop back toward or onto your heels while releasing your forehead onto the floor, a pillow, or your stacked palms.

3. Rest in this position for two to five minutes, allowing your body to deeply relax and release unnecessary tensions.

4. **Alternatively:** Place a small pillow or folded towel on a table (or desk). Sit in a chair facing the table, and then rest your forehead on the pillow/towel with your arms also supported by the table.

3
NOVEMBER
—

There are three jewels that I cherish:
compassion, moderation, and humility.

TAO TE CHING, **CHAPTER 67**

4
NOVEMBER
—
TURTLE WISDOM

When a turtle is active, its motto is "Slow and steady gets the job done." And when protection and/or solitude is necessary, the turtle withdraws into its shell. Be willing, when it's appropriate, to apply turtle wisdom to your life.

5

NOVEMBER

FORGIVENESS #2

1. Sit comfortably or lie down; then gently close your eyes.

2. Bring to mind something that you did or said that you regret but now are ready to forgive.

3. Imagine a miniature version of yourself (no more than an inch tall) in the form of light, like a little fairy.

4. Imagine this fairylike version of yourself floating in your lower *tan-t'ien* or heart-center, whichever you'd prefer.

5. In whatever way makes sense to you, ask for or offer forgiveness, and imagine the tiny light-being version of yourself gratefully receiving or willingly offering it.

6. To end the exercise, allow the light being to dissolve and merge with the light of your heart-center or lower *tan-t'ien*.

6
NOVEMBER

TEARS AND LAUGHTER

Intimately experience the full range of emotions, but let them flow through
without rejecting, magnifying, or holding on to them. Be like a young child who
cries after skinning their knee but five minutes later is laughing again.

7
NOVEMBER

CH'I-KUNG AND MEDITATION

Movement cultivates fire energy. Stillness and quietude nourish water energy.
Ch'i-kung practice is the external expression of movement and energy. Meditation is the internal enjoyment of quietude.

Like dance partners, they work together beautifully to support health
and vitality.

The "Te" of *Tao Te Ching* is often translated as "virtue," though it also refers to:

(A) The manifestation of the Tao within all things.

(B) An inner power, integrity, and heartfelt authenticity that arises spontaneously when you're in alignment with the Tao.

When you're "holding to the One," your thoughts, words, and actions are naturally virtuous because the power and clarity of the Tao flow transparently through your human body-mind. When you're in perfect harmony with your original nature, *te* shines through all your worldly activities.

In the coming weeks, notice how your actions effortlessly align with your understanding, how "doing the right thing" just happens naturally.

9
NOVEMBER

—

If you want to become whole,
first let yourself become broken.
If you want to become straight,
first let yourself become twisted.
If you want to become full,
first let yourself become empty.

TAO TE CHING, **CHAPTER 22**

10
NOVEMBER

—

FREE AND MYSTERIOUS

All things share a common origin: the Tao. Yet they also appear, through our human cognitive-perceptual faculties, as being separate.

In truth, phenomena can never be captured by dualistic concepts of same/different or separate/identical. They remain free and mysterious.

NOVEMBER

FINGERS INTERLACED

1. Lie down on the floor or recline on a couch or easy chair.

2. If you'd like, support your head with a pillow.

3. Interlace your fingers behind your head and allow your elbows to drop wide, like a butterfly opening its wings. If your head is supported by a pillow, you can interlace your fingers either underneath or on top of it.

4. Take a few deep, slow breaths, drawing the inhalation into the space between your shoulder blades. As you exhale, say "ahh" to help relax your face, neck, and jaw.

5. Gently close your eyes. Fully surrender the weight of your body to the floor or chair. Remain for two to five minutes.

12
NOVEMBER
—
NEVER TWICE

A flowing river is always subtly unique, never identical to the previous moment.
So the only way to really know a river is to experience it directly, to let it flow through your fingers or swim in it or drink its water, here and now.

13
NOVEMBER
—
MICROBIOME

Your human body is in a symbiotic relationship with a multitude of friendly bacteria: the microbiome. Remember this when contemplating your body: It's not a singular entity, but rather a whole community!

It's also wise to keep these microflora happy with probiotic foods: yogurt, kefir, miso, tempeh, sauerkraut, kimchi, kombucha.

14
NOVEMBER
—
HONOR YOUR SCARS

Love and celebrate your scars and wounded places as emblems of the adventures and challenges that your body-mind has encountered.

Seeming imperfections (birthmarks, blemishes, and scars) are nothing to be ashamed of. They're simply part of your uniqueness.

Though harmony and balance are Taoist ideals, perfect symmetry doesn't exist in the natural world, so don't expect it of your human body-mind.

A gnarled and knotted tree, a flower with half its petals blown off in the wind, a buck that has lost one of his horns are all beautiful in their own way.

Understand that true perfection never lies in a form, no matter how sublime, but only in the Light of Tao.

15
NOVEMBER

If you invest everything in something that, by nature, is unstable, while there is nothing wrong with doing so, you must acknowledge that one day, you will have to let it go.

—SHI HENG YI, SHAOLIN TEMPLE EUROPE

16
NOVEMBER

ENJOY THE SHOW

You enjoy a magic show without believing it to be real. It's fun not knowing the magician's secrets because then you can feel astonished, delighted, bewildered, and amazed.

The events of the cosmos are a fantastic magic show.

17

NOVEMBER

TOES AND HEELS

1. Sit on the edge of a chair with your feet hip-distance apart.

2. Lift the toes of both feet strongly with your heels still anchored on the floor, flexing your ankles.

3. Reverse this action by lifting your heels while the base of your toes remains anchored on the floor, lengthening the front of both ankles.

4. Move back and forth a dozen times or so, keeping your spine upright.

5. With an inhale, open your arms wide as you lift your toes, as though gathering energy from the cosmos. And with the exhale, press your forearms toward one another as you lift your heels, drawing that energy into the central channel.

18

NOVEMBER

LONGEVITY

Li Ching-Yuen was a legendary Taoist practitioner who, through *ch'i-kung* practice and powerful herbal formulas, achieved remarkable longevity, living to be around 200 years old!

Do you have an aspiration for physical longevity? If so, why?

19

NOVEMBER

CURIOSITY

When faced with differing opinions and on the precipice of conflict, shift into curiosity: *I wonder how they've reached this conclusion. I wonder why they feel so strongly about it.*

And ask the same questions about your own beliefs and opinions.

20
NOVEMBER

OPTIONS

If inspired, experiment over the next couple of weeks with these healthy substitutions:

- Instead of reaching for a soda, enjoy a mug of kombucha with live active probiotic cultures.

- Instead of alcohol, relax with some chamomile tea or celery juice—both natural sedatives.

- Instead of a candy bar, reach for some dried apricots, figs, or dates to satisfy your sweet tooth.

- Instead of downing your third cup of coffee, enjoy a matcha latte or a cup of chai.

Track the effects of these changes in your journal, if you keep one. Otherwise, just tune into how you're feeling to decide if the new habit is worth keeping.

21
NOVEMBER

VISION

When, in shifting clouds, you see an animal or an angel, is this a mirror of your mind's personal patterns? Or a reflection of the collective unconscious of humanity? Or a genuine revelation: a form of prophecy?

22
NOVEMBER

GOLDEN LIGHT FLOWING #2

1. Stand or sit comfortably.

2. Rub the palms of your hands together for fifteen to twenty seconds.

3. Float your left palm a couple inches away from your torso at the level of your lower left rib cage, where your spleen is located.

4. At the same time, float your right hand six to eight inches away from your lower abdomen, with the center of your palm pointing toward your lower *tan-t'ien*.

5. With your hands in this position, imagine a stream of golden light flowing from your spleen to your lower *tan-t'ien*.

6. Continue for one to two minutes, and then rest both palms gently on your lower *tan-t'ien* for a few breaths.

23
NOVEMBER
———

Water is the softest and most yielding substance.
Yet nothing is better than water,
for overcoming the hard and rigid,
because nothing can compete with it.

TAO TE CHING, **CHAPTER 78**

24
NOVEMBER
—
WORD DANCE

In the Taoist art form of calligraphy, word creation becomes a physical as well as mental activity. Even after the ink has dried, the words seem to dance on the canvas.

Their visual beauty is an essential aspect of their meaning.

25
NOVEMBER
—
ORDINARY AND EXTRAORDINARY

Find the extraordinary in the ordinary.

For any object or event, contemplate all the causes and conditions that had to come together for it to manifest. Understand that, ultimately, it's the entire universe colluding to appear as trees, mountains, ladybugs, hurricanes, and humans, like the ocean appearing as waves of various sizes, shapes, and colors.

Honor each member of the plant, mineral, animal, and fungi kingdoms as a living being with its own wisdom and perhaps also personality, wit, and playfulness. Be curious about what this wisdom might be.

And be open to the possibility that the essence of your seemingly ordinary mind is all-pervading, eternal Being Awareness: the Light of Tao.

26
NOVEMBER

—

RELATIONS

How would your relationship with other people, and all living beings, change if you knew without a doubt that the Awareness flowing through their eyes and your eyes was not separate but rather the one Light of Tao?

27
NOVEMBER
—

THE MOODS OF MOTHER NATURE

The regal quietude of a redwood forest.
  The explosive power of a volcanic eruption.
  The immensity of a galaxy.
  The audacious colors of a coral reef.
  Mother nature has so many moods!

28
NOVEMBER
—

IN SILENT TRANQUILITY

Liu I-Ming (translated by Thomas Cleary) has written:

"Perfected human beings transform the temporal and restore the primal. They rest their bodies in open space, store their spirits in silent tranquility. Uninvolved with the energy of the five forces, they are unmoved by myriad things. They have no smoke, no fire, like deadwood or cold ashes; they have no form, no shape, like the sky or a valley. Heaven and earth cannot constrain them, Creation cannot rule them."

Explore this passage more deeply by contemplating:

- What does it mean to rest the body in open space?

- What does it mean to store the spirit in silent tranquility?

- What does it mean for a perfected human being to have no form or shape?

29
NOVEMBER
—

In a hundred years, everyone we know will be just a pile of bones. What is there to gain in life, and what is there to lose in death?

—LIEH-TZU (TRANSLATED BY EVA WONG, *LIEH-TZU: A TAOIST GUIDE TO PRACTICAL LIVING*)

30
NOVEMBER
—

ETERNAL AND DEATHLESS

The body is born and dies.
    The Tao is eternal and deathless.
    Time and space, and the ten thousand things, appear within it.
    So what is your true identity: the ephemeral body-mind or the eternal Tao?

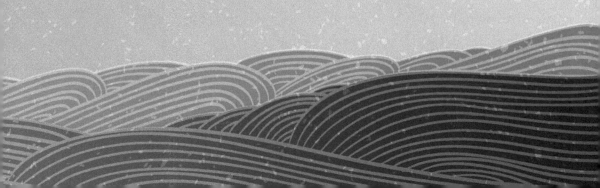

DECEMBER

1
DECEMBER
SACRED TURTLE

Chuang Tzu once asked: Is it better to be a sacred turtle—dead for three thousand years and displayed on the altar of a prince—or a turtle alive and wagging its tail in the mud?

Which would you choose?

2
DECEMBER
THREE ADVISERS

The Taoist three *tan-t'iens* are a bit like three brains: three centers of intelligence. Interestingly, modern science has confirmed that neural tissue exists not only in the brain but also in the heart and in the gastrointestinal tract.

To consult the wisdom of each of the *tan-t'iens*, as trusted advisers:

1. Clearly formulate your question or concern, and write it down.

2. Sit comfortably or lie down.

3. With your question in mind, rest your attention in the lower *tan-t'ien* (the deep belly). Listen for an answer in the form of images, words, or sensations.

4. Repeat this process with your attention resting in the middle (center-chest) and upper (center-head) *tan-t'iens*.

3
DECEMBER
———
LEMONADE

If you vividly imagine biting into a slice of lemon, chances are good that you'll begin to salivate. This shows the power of imagination—of your mind—to influence your body.

Be curious about how ephemeral thoughts can affect presumably dense matter.

4
DECEMBER
—

WHICH IS BIGGER: THE UNIVERSE OR A PEA?

1. As you eat, notice the various shapes, colors, scents, and textures of the food.

2. Every now and again, just for fun, address one of the foods by name, and trace its genealogy: all the causes and conditions that came together to create it.

3. For instance: "Hello, pea, and welcome to my plate. Let's see who inhabits your ancestral tree: soil (with all its minerals), sunshine, rain, the workers who harvested you," and so on.

4. See that it's the entire universe that has come together to produce this tiny pea and to nourish your human body. How amazing! Each bite is the universe!

5

DECEMBER

Humanity follows the earth.
Earth follows Heaven.
Heaven follows the Tao.
The Tao follows only itself.

TAO TE CHING, **CHAPTER 25**

6

DECEMBER

NOT-TWO

Waves are expressions of ocean water, and ocean water is the substance of each wave. Just so, Tao and the ten thousand things are not-two.

Similarly, awareness and humanity are not-two. Appreciate and honor your humanity, precisely because it is an expression of the Divine.

7
DECEMBER

MICROCOSMIC ORBIT

1. Sit comfortably with your spine upright.

2. Touch the tip of your tongue lightly to the roof of your mouth behind your upper front teeth.

3. With each inhale, feel your lower *tan-t'ien* filling with golden-white light. With the exhale, enjoy any sensations of warmth or tingling. Continue for ten cycles of the breath.

4. As you exhale, imagine this energy of your lower *tan-t'ien* flowing down to Hui Yin (the center of your pelvic floor).

5. With the next inhale, draw this energy into your tailbone and then up your spine all the way to the center of your brain.

6. With the next exhalation, feel it flowing like a waterfall, down the center-line of your face and front torso, back into the space of the lower *tan-t'ien*.

8
DECEMBER
WELCOMING

To welcome the totality of your experience (perceptions, sensations, and thoughts) doesn't necessarily mean taking or not taking action. It means allowing the most wise and efficient action to spontaneously emerge, as the impersonal activity of the You-niverse.

9
DECEMBER
SKY GAZING

As inspired, simply gaze at a clear blue sky. Allow your view to be soft and wide. Feel yourself becoming as vast and spacious as the sky. Let your entire being merge with its pristine clarity. Say "ahh."

10
DECEMBER

I AM NOT MOVING

1. Sit comfortably, with your palms resting on your thighs. Close your eyes.

2. Allow just one of your fingers to move up and down, tapping it lightly on your thigh.

3. Say to yourself, "My finger is moving, and I am not moving." Find the "place" from which this statement is true.

4. Allow one of your hands to move in small circles. Say to yourself, "My hand is moving, and I am not moving." Find the "place" from which this statement is true.

5. Gently rotate your head, and say to yourself, "My head is moving, and I am not moving." Find the "place" from which this statement is true.

11

DECEMBER

—

Being one with Tao, we are no longer concerned about losing our life because we know the Tao is constant and we are one with Tao.

TAO TE CHING, **CHAPTER 16**

12

DECEMBER

—

AIKIDO WISDOM

With circling and spiraling movements, an Aikido master turns the momentum of an attack back against their opponent.

Becoming one with the "enemy," they're able, with power and subtlety, to radically transform the contours of the encounter.

13
DECEMBER

MEETING OF HEAVEN AND EARTH #3

1. Stand with your feet shoulder-width apart.

2. Float your hands in front of your chest with palms facing one another about ten inches apart and your fingers slightly separated and relaxed.

3. Imagine you're holding a sphere of light between your palms.

4. With an exhale, press your right palm up toward the sky and your left palm down toward the earth.

5. With the next inhale, bring your palms back to facing in front of your chest.

6. With the next exhale, press your left palm up toward the sky and your right palm down toward the earth.

7. With the next inhale, bring your palms back to center-chest.

8. Repeat this cycle six to eight times.

14
DECEMBER
—

WAITING WITHOUT WAITING

An innocent sense of expectation—*I wonder what's going to happen next*—can arise within relaxed contentment.

Already satisfied, already at ease, yet imbued with the vital curiosity of a young child, you observe the transformations of the ten thousand things.

15
DECEMBER
—

CAVE

A cave can be dark for a thousand years, but the moment a lamp is lit, the cave is filled with light.

One moment of seeing your true nature can put an end to ignorance and psychological suffering.

16
DECEMBER

MICRO-MEDITATION

Sometimes, very brief meditation sessions, several times during the day, can be just as effective as a single longer session.

For instance:

- While sitting at your desk at work, close your eyes and tune into the movement of your breath for just thirty seconds.

- Pause whatever you're doing and gaze for a moment at the sky, say "ahh," and enter the space of not-knowing.

- In the midst of chaotic activity, remind yourself that who you are essentially is the observing Awareness—silent and unmoving.

This homeopathic approach to meditation and inquiry can be surprisingly effective, a powerful way to facilitate glimpses into your true nature.

17
DECEMBER
—

The Tao of Heaven nourishes by not forcing.
The Tao of the Wise person acts by not competing.

TAO TE CHING, **CHAPTER 81**

18
DECEMBER
—
SELF-FORGIVENESS

All forgiveness is Self-forgiveness: *giving back* to the Tao—to the Divine—what you've labeled as a problem.

It's surrendering the entire situation and trusting its resolution to the One who ultimately created it.

19
DECEMBER

—

DRAWING A BOW AND ARROW

1. Stand with your feet shoulder-width apart.

2. Float your hands in front of your chest, palms facing one another.

3. With an exhale, press your left palm strongly to the left at shoulder height, with the palm stretched open and fingers separated. At the same time, curl your right fingers into a loose fist, and pull this fist (leading with your right elbow) slightly to the right, as though you were drawing a bow in preparation for shooting an arrow.

4. With an inhale, bring your hands back to center.

5. On the next exhale, draw the bow in the other direction.

6. Inhale back to center.

20
DECEMBER

PERSISTENCE

For six million years, the Colorado River streamed and flowed, trickled and surged, gushed and eddied, and meandered. The result was the Grand Canyon.

Did it plan to create this magnificent canyon? In its own way of expressing itself, this is just what happened.

21
DECEMBER

HEAVEN IN THE PALM OF YOUR HAND

1. Sit comfortably.

2. Turn your left palm to face upward.

3. At the same time, turn your right palm to face your lower *tan-t'ien*, six to eight inches away.

4. Imagine the energy of Heaven—the sun, moon, stars, and galaxies—flowing into your left palm. Feel it gathering there, like a pool of warm water or a sphere of light.

5. Allow this Heaven-energy to flow up your left arm into the armpit, then into your heart-center, then into your right armpit, down your right arm into your right hand, and from there into your lower *tan-t'ien*.

6. Feel the warmth and brightness of Heaven-energy gathering in your lower *tan-t'ien*.

22
DECEMBER
———

How does the Sage seat himself by the sun and moon, and hold the universe in his grasp? He blends everything into one harmonious whole, rejecting the confusion of this and that.

—CHUANG TZU (TRANSLATED BY HERBERT GILES)

23
DECEMBER

UNDERGROUND NETWORK

Both the mycelium of mushrooms and the roots of aspen trees form intercon-nected matrices—underground networks of communication that allow them to function as a single organism.

Can you feel a similar connection with all-that-is?

24
DECEMBER

LAZY DAY

1. In the true spirit of the Sabbath, enjoy a lazy day, where nothing at all is planned in advance.

2. When you wake up, ask yourself, *What would I like to do now?*

3. Enjoy that activity, and when it has reached its natural conclusion, ask the same question, *What would I like to do now?*

4. Maybe the next activity will be a nap, maybe it will be to go for a long run. Maybe to practice calligraphy or go shopping or visit a museum or meet a friend for lunch.

5. Continue in this fashion, spontaneously following your enthusiasm, from moment to moment.

25
DECEMBER

WILDFLOWERS

Like wildflowers on the meadow, each human being is a unique expression of the Divine, the Tao.

Celebrate yourself, and others, for this uniqueness at the level of form while remaining aware of our shared essence.

26
DECEMBER

FLOWING INTO THE GAP

1. Sit comfortably or lie down.

2. Bring your attention to the movement of your breath: the cycling of the inhales and exhales.

3. Become interested in the gap between the inhale and the exhale and between the exhale and the inhale.

4. Let your attention flow into these gaps, experiencing them more intimately.

5. Without creating any extra tension, allow these gaps to expand, with the next inhale or exhale just emerging on its own, naturally.

6. Can you draw the essence of the still, silent gap into each inhalation and exhalation, like an infant drawing milk from their mother's breast? Be curious about this possibility.

27

DECEMBER

FLOAT

In the womb-like silence and complete darkness of a flotation tank, with only the sounds of your breathing and heartbeat, the memory of being in your mother's womb may well be resurrected.

Are you ready?

28

DECEMBER

SOUND INTO SILENCE

1. Let a sound ring out; you can use a singing bowl, a bell, a tuning fork, or something virtual online. Follow the sound into silence.

2. Rest in this silence. Feel its shimmering vitality, its luminosity. It's not a dead, inert silence. It's who you are, most essentially.

3. Be curious: Does this silence have a center or periphery? Can you find its edges?

4. Be nourished by the silence. Feel it permeating your human body. Feel it as a soothing balm for your mind—just resting here in silence.

5. Then, when you're ready, sound the bell again, and once again follow it into silence.

Be grateful to the sound for taking you to the silence of your true nature, like a taxi taking you to a party.

29
DECEMBER

METAMORPHOSIS

When a caterpillar disappears behind the wall of the chrysalis, apparently dead to the world of caterpillars, does it really die?

When you realize your true nature, you are like the butterfly. And your wingspan is the entire cosmos.

30
DECEMBER

The Tao is nearby, yet people seek wonderful doctrines far away.

—**LIU I-MING** (TRANSLATED BY THOMAS CLEARY IN *AWAKENING TO THE TAO*)

31
DECEMBER

UNCHANGING LIGHT

Buds in spring, fruit in summer's harvest, beautiful leaves in autumn, and winter's hibernation, which gives birth to next spring's buds.

Celebrate these cycles, and know yourself as the unchanging Light of Tao within which they playfully appear.

RESOURCES

CLASSIC TEXTS

Find translations of Lao Tzu's *Tao Te Ching* and Chuang Tzu's *Chuang Tzu* that appeal to you. These are the foundational texts of Classical Taoism and great to have on hand and return to often.

EXCELLENT FOR BEGINNERS

The Art of Writing: Teachings of the Chinese Masters, translated by Tony Barnstone and Chou Ping. Playful and profound verses and commentaries.

Awakening to the Tao by Liu I-Ming. Delightful meditative essays that illustrate how a renowned Taoist adept uses the events of daily life to cultivate the Mind of Tao.

The Book of the Heart: Embracing the Tao by Loy Ching-Yuen. Concise poetic verses, each offering an insightful reflection on some aspect of Taoist practice.

Lieh-Tzu: A Taoist Guide to Practical Living by Eva Wong. Stories, meditative musings, and friendly advice attributed to the Taoist sage Lieh-Tzu.

Opening the Dragon Gate: The Making of a Modern Taoist Wizard by Chen Kaiguo and Zheng Shunchao. An engaging tale of the training of a Taoist adept.

Road to Heaven: Encounters with Chinese Hermits by Red Pine. Meetings with contemporary Taoist and Buddhist hermits.

The Secret of the Golden Flower by Thomas Cleary. A classic Taoist meditation manual, attributed to Taoist sage Lu Tung-pin, that explains the practice of "turning the light around."

The Way of Energy: Mastering the Chinese Art of Internal Strength with Chi Kung Exercise by Lam Kam Chuen. An excellent introduction to the Taoist practice of standing meditation.

FOR THE ADVENTUROUS
All Else Is Bondage: Non-Volitional Living by Wei Wu Wei. Taoist wisdom in a Western idiom, written in a Chuang Tzu–like style: playful dialogues and vignettes pointing to the Tao, like a finger pointing to the moon.

FOR INCREASED KNOWLEDGE
Enteric nervous system: "The Brain-Gut Connection." Johns Hopkins Medicine. hopkinsmedicine.org/health/wellness-and-prevention /the-brain-gut-connection.

Herbal intestinal cleanse: See Dr. Natura's website: drnatura.com /cleansing-health-benefits.

Neural tissue in the heart: See the HeartMath Institute's website: heartmath .org/our-heart-brain.

REFERENCES

Anderton, Kate. "What Are Mirror Neurons?" *News-Medical*, February 27, 2019. news-medical.net/health/What-are-Mirror-Neurons.aspx.

Chia, Mantak. *The Six Healing Sounds: Taoist Techniques for Balancing Chi.* Rochester: Destiny Books, 2009.

Hewlings, Susan J., and Douglas S. Kalman. "Curcumin: A Review of Its Effects on Human Health." *Foods* 6, no. 10 (October 2017): 92.

Reninger, Elizabeth. "Acupressure of Hui Yin Point." *Learn Religions*, March 14, 2019. learnreligions.com/acupressure-treasures-hui-yin-ren-1-3182278.

Riggio, Ronald E. "There's Magic in Your Smile: How Smiling Affects Your Brain." *Psychology Today*, June 25, 2012. psychologytoday.com/us/blog/cutting-edge-leadership/201206/there-s-magic-in-your-smile.

Selig, Meg. "The 9 Superpowers of Your Smile." *Psychology Today*, May 25, 2016. psychologytoday.com/us/blog/changepower/201605/the-9-superpowers-your-smile.

ACKNOWLEDGMENTS

While the actual writing of a book is often a solitary activity, its images and ideas necessarily emerge from a rich network of influences. Naming every one of these influences would clearly be impossible, but I do wish to acknowledge—with deep bows of gratitude—the following people:

My mother, whose lifelong interest in nutrition and *t'ai-chi* to support health and well-being sowed fertile seeds.

James MacRitchie, Eva Wong, Charles Chase, and Li Junfeng, for inspiring *ch'i-kung* instruction.

Francis Lucille, for nourishing and clarifying my passion for nondual spiritual inquiry, which provides the spark for creative endeavors such as this one.

And finally, deepest appreciation for mystic poets—past, present, and future—whose playful-serious speaking of the unspeakable remains an eternal source of inspiration.

ABOUT THE AUTHOR

Elizabeth Reninger is a practitioner of the Taoist arts of *ch'i-kung*, meditation, and poetry. She holds an MS in Chinese Medicine and has explored and written widely on topics related to nondual spiritual traditions. Her previous books include *And Now the Story Lives Inside You*, *Meditation Now*, and *Taoism for Beginners*. Elizabeth currently lives, works, and plays in Boulder, Colorado.

CPSIA information can be obtained
at www.ICGtesting.com
Printed in the USA
JSHW041953101022
31518JS00004B/7